REAL
FREEDOM

WHY FRANCHISES ARE WORTH CONSIDERING AND HOW THEY CAN BE USED FOR BUILDING WEALTH

REAL
FREEDOM

WHY FRANCHISES ARE WORTH
CONSIDERING AND HOW THEY CAN
BE USED FOR BUILDING WEALTH

GREGORY K. MOHR
FRANCHISE MAVEN

Published by Best Seller Publishing®, St. Augustine, FL
Best Seller Publishing® is a registered trademark.
Printed in the United States of America.
ISBN: 978-1-956649-45-1

For more information, please write:
Best Seller Publishing®
53 Marine St
St. Augustine, FL 32084
or call 1 (626) 765-9750
Visit us online at: www.BestSellerPublishing.org

DISCLAIMER:

This information is not intended as an offer to sell
or the solicitation of an offer to buy a franchise.
It is for informational purposes only.

PRAISE FOR GREG MOHR AND FRANCHISE MAVEN

Greg is amazing! He helped me to find the right franchise in such a short time. His advice was always helpful. I enjoyed working with him, and I really recommend his expertise. I couldn't imagine a better franchise consultant!

NOURHEN HAOUAS
FINANCE DIRECTOR, ECE

If you are looking for a partner to walk you through life as a franchisee, the opportunities, mitigating challenges, understanding fit, STOP looking. Greg's your guy!

LON KREGER, MSBA
CHIEF COMMERCIAL OFFICER, MAGGROW

I cannot speak highly enough about Greg. He was always so professional while connecting and truly understanding of what I was looking for. His approach screams that he cares, which is very encouraging considering he is helping most to start a new career. He is genuine, diligent, and well thought out. He asked great questions and provided great solutions, never missing a beat. I truly appreciate the time Greg put into our search and would highly recommend him to anyone looking for a franchise/new business opportunity.

STEVE SCIORTINO
PARTNER & RELATIONSHIP MANAGER,
PARK CEDAR LENDING

Hey, anyone looking for help in finding a franchise please reach out to Greg. He was extremely helpful in guiding me to the right business. Greg was able to answer all my questions and even had recommendations to someone who could help if he did not have an answer. It was a pleasure working with Greg throughout the process of purchasing my first franchise.

CHARLES ZANGER JR.
FRANCHISE OWNER,
MEINEKE CAR CARE CENTERS, INC.

Gregory K. Mohr was a great guy to work with.

ANTHONY HAMM
SEMICONDUCTORS PROFESSIONAL

TABLE OF CONTENTS

INTRODUCTION

Before we get started, here's a little bit of background about who I am and what I have done in my past to bring me to this point in life where I am writing a book on franchising. I got my start right out of high school as a restaurant manager for a fast-food chain. That's when I got my first actual look at franchising. I worked for a master franchisor of Taco Bell throughout the Sacramento area, helping the restaurants grow and become more profitable.

First, I want to address the fact that not all franchises are restaurants; it's just where I happened to get my first look. Overall, I really enjoyed the fact that established restaurants had all the systems and processes in place. As I was helping the master franchisor with managing some of her locations and day-to-day tasks, I quickly learned all the procedures. The procedures made it very easy to train people; you knew who you needed and when you needed them.

With the restaurant business, there are certain times of day, obviously, that are busier than others. We knew, based on sales, exactly how many employees we needed and what locations they were needed in, which made for very simple operations. It all felt so logical to me, and it felt really good to be able to walk into any of the Taco Bells in the Sacramento area and know that I'd be doing the exact same things no matter the location.

As I traveled the region, there was only one bad thing I noticed when I walked into these different restaurants. There were certain managers who had been there before me, and they weren't exactly following those policies and procedures. Maybe they thought they knew better. Nevertheless, they were making changes here and there—and those decisions weren't paying off.

I was actually placed at those locations to put everything back on track, to make them run smoothly and efficiently according to the policies and procedures that Taco Bell had outlined. I learned that if you're a new manager, your first day is not the right time to try to make improvements to proven systems and processes. Spend the time needed to get them in place, and then spend the time to maintain the right results. Later, when you're a top owner, you might be able to add new ideas. There is room for growth, but you should get to know the improvement process first and foremost.

As a teenager, I definitely saw that franchising was a great option. I would later learn much more about it (especially that it's not limited to restaurants), but I'm grateful for my first experience in the franchise world.

I then moved on to a 24-hour food chain, Lyons, which is similar to Denny's. Then, after seven teen years in the food service business, it was time for something else, so I went to school and became an engineer. I received my degree in electrical engineering and physics at Sacramento State University and went to work for Motorola's semiconductor division. While working, I also received an MBA in management information systems and read a lot of business books. I thought I would be able to advance my corporate career by doing so. It turns out I didn't, but I learned a lot of valuable information I would use later.

Being in the corporate world, I found I was always working on somebody else's terms. I wanted to work on my own terms. When you have your own business, you're doing everything on your terms and building it up for yourself. Everyone is trying to build better lives for themselves and their families. That's really what drove me into looking to do franchising and ultimately getting out of my corporate job and buying a franchise.

I have a trusted team, and we have some real-world pictures of what people have done working with me and working with a franchise consultant.

We're going to go through the greatest plan for building wealth in franchising, the investment levels of time and money, and what financing options are available to you. We'll go through the six processes of investing, step by step, and what to look for in a franchise, which ties into what you might expect to get out of one.

My motivation is to help others. I was helping a lot of people when I was an engineer. I was helping a lot of engineers and was doing quite a bit of training. I've always liked to help people. I'll explain to you as we go through the book how I found the franchise consultant who would help me find a franchise for myself that I felt good about. My motivation has become taking you through the process of what I did to find a franchise that supported me in achieving my freedom, and to help you achieve yours.

There are many different franchises out there that require different amounts of your time—passive, semi-passive, and full-time—and you'll have the freedom to decide what fits you best. That's the whole idea behind franchising and owning your own business—you've got the freedom to decide what you want to do. Throughout this book, my ambition has been to make all of this simpler for you to figure out which franchise is best for you.

When you actually get into franchising and you're following the corporation's policies and procedures, you discover a certain freedom in the existing structure. You know their preference, you know what you want outside of the business, and as long as you stay within their guidelines, it's still your business. Where I am now, I don't necessarily need to be at any one spot at any one time; I can do the things I want to do throughout the day. Even working for Taco Bell, once the employees were trained and everything was running like clockwork according to the policies and procedures, I could see how the franchisee could step away. That was never the case in the corporate world.

At my traditional job, I could never just walk away. If they didn't see me at my desk—if I was taking a longer lunch than they wanted or using the restroom at the wrong time—I was bad. That earned me a demerit. I didn't get my star for the day. Basically, whatever I was doing was immaterial. They needed to see me there, and if they didn't, that worked against the way they saw me as an employee.

Franchisees have real freedom. You can come and go as you please and do what you please throughout the day. As long as everything is running the way it's supposed to be running—which is easy to follow with guidelines—your day is entirely up to you. As long as the systems are working, the business is coming in steadily, and you're growing that business, there are no demerits for living the life you want.

When I was a newcomer, I took the time I needed to get in touch with everything. Eventually, I could tell that I could take extra time off without any guilt or worry. Sure, I would do some extra work here and there, but that was to secure the life I dreamed of down the line. I could walk away. My employees were doing everything they were supposed to be doing. I knew things were running smoothly. I just needed to come back and check on everything occasionally to ensure things were going right. And I would know how to correct errors because I had the structures and guidelines.

Do you want a life where nobody is standing over your shoulder, looking at you, and asking, "Why aren't you at your desk?" I know I didn't like that atmosphere. Given the choice, that's a No for me. And I imagine that's a No for you, too. Say Yes to freedom.

Much in the way I work with my clients, over the course of my book I'll take you through the process. I believe I can help you understand yourself as well, more than ever before. You know what past experiences you have had that will help you determine which franchise is a great one for you. We're looking for you to understand what it is you're trying to accomplish. Ultimately, this is all about launching your dream of total independence or of having more retirement funds, time with your family, or whatever that dream may be; we're going to get you there through this book.

At any time while reading this book, don't hesitate to go to my website franchisemaven.com. My contact information is there. You can schedule time with me, and we'll get started going through the process together.

CHAPTER 1

FREEDOM IS ONE FRANCHISE AWAY

Over the years I worked for other people, but I knew that there had to be a better way. Straight out of high school, I started working for a master franchisor (an entrepreneur who purchases exclusive rights to a large regional territory, wherein the master recruits new franchisees and helps them open their locations) for Taco Bell, as I mentioned in the Introduction. Boy, that was quite a while ago! While I searched for work, I took a look at a couple of different restaurants before I applied. They were all corporate-type restaurants with corporate-style structures—I didn't necessarily care for them. Subconsciously, I knew there was a better way; however, I didn't know what that was just yet.

I think everybody wants to be appreciated, and I did at the time. Within that franchise environment, before I became a manager, I remember walking through one location in particular with the master franchisor, and I could tell how happy everyone was to be there. They really enjoyed what they were doing. They really had a good time with it. I knew it when I saw it: that was exactly the kind of environment I wanted.

Obviously, making a living requires exchanging work for money, but it doesn't necessarily need to be *tedious* work that's not appreciated or enjoyable. Leo, the master franchisor, was setting up locations where employees were having fun and getting everything done, and they efficiently completed the day and made their customers happy. There wasn't a lot of stress, and people genuinely had a great time. They knew what the guidelines were, and how they needed to dress and present themselves, and none of this seemed to affect their day negatively. It seemed rare at the time.

I've always been a man who looks for challenges—so I didn't stay an employee at Taco Bell for too long. I became manager before I even graduated high school. One of the greatest things I did as a high school student was skip a week of classes in order to manage multiple restaurants in Davis, California, while their manager was away on vacation. Oh my gosh! It was the coolest thing in the whole wide world. Then again, maybe this isn't something I'm supposed to brag about today ...

But really, being able to say I was too busy to do the things that everyone else needed to do was fulfilling to me as a teenager. It was a good challenge, being the one in charge—the one whom everybody looked to. I was responsible for making certain that the restaurants ran the way they should, and I hadn't even graduated yet. It was a challenge and I like challenges, which the master franchisor provided me.

Eventually, I thought I might try the challenges of semi-casual dining. I found an opportunity with the Lyons restaurant chain in Northern California (think Denny's if you haven't heard of it). I reset my path and worked as a waiter first, and then I leveled up to management again. I ran one restaurant for a while and then moved around to other locations as a general manager.

I was running into the same wall. It always reached a point where there weren't enough challenges for me. At the end of the day, I was always working for somebody, but I certainly appreciated the structures and systems in place. Specific to Lyons, I think it got old for me just because there were long hours from it being open twenty-four hours a day. There was always something going on, and I thought I might do better with a different schedule and a different path—something out of the food industry, perhaps.

The more I thought about it, the more I knew that I wanted something different. Well, I was good at engineering and math and in truth, my family had a certain legacy with regard to engineering—primarily, my sister was a chemical engineer and my father was a mechanical engineer. It seemed like the right thing to do, so I decided that would be my next step.

A BLESSING IN DISGUISE

After about fifteen years in food service, and much of that in management, I demoted myself back to being a waiter. I went to school, got degrees in electrical engineering and physics, and I became a microelectronic circuit engineer. I did that for a while, fifteen years, but while I discovered that I generally liked helping others, over time, the job as an engineer wasn't fulfilling enough for me.

My first corporate job was in Austin, Texas, at Motorola Semiconductor. It was so awesome to me when I started! It was a great job, and I loved it. But then the corporate thing started setting in. After a while, corporate was just looking over my shoulder and I was just making sure I was seen at my desk all the time. The atmosphere was getting tedious, but I really liked the challenges that came my way in the work itself.

So far, the pattern was that there were great new challenges every time I stepped into something different. That's what I look for as far as moving up in my career is concerned. As I started feeling the tediousness of it all, I decided to find new challenges outside work by way of earning my master's degree. My thought was that I would move up the corporate ladder, which is why I chose a business master's—I later realized I could have been paid more if I had chosen engineering again.

While I was living the corporate life, I was reading Robert Kiyosaki's books. He writes some good ones, and I remain a fan today (if you haven't already done so, I encourage you to look into his book *Rich Dad, Poor Dad*). Later on, I was also reading books by Zig Ziglar, who writes a lot about sales. He once wrote, "You can get what you want in life. If you help enough people get what they want in life." These influential figures probably ruined corporate life for me, on a certain level. Overall, it was still encouraging to know that there was indeed a better way.

Before I finished my master's degree, I thought I might return to my old roots. In the interest of keeping things a little more interesting, a fellow engineer and I purchased a dry-cleaning business with several drop-off locations, and one location had storage units as well. I also bought some rental properties, which I very much liked handling. A little problem with me (and the problem with a lot of folks) was that I needed to take a closer look at what was driving me to do something different. Well, a great opportunity to do exactly that presented itself.

The day eventually arrived when my bosses figured out what I was figuring out: my heart was just not in the corporate job. I was laid off. For some people, that's probably the deciding factor. A big change like that happens, and then it's time to just take a look at your life, see how it's been going, and see what needs changing. For me, I decided that I never wanted to work for another person again. Moving forward, I would only work for myself.

I knew from great minds like Kiyosaki and Ziglar that if I wanted to help as many people as I could, the corporate world simply would not cut it for me. I needed something more. I already knew that franchising was a good option (and I can tell you today that it definitely is). I researched more businesses and started learning what it would take to do franchising well. I invested in a telecommunications consulting franchise, and I haven't looked back since.

In truth, getting laid off was a blessing in disguise. I found myself somewhat reborn in the world again, helping many businesses with their telecommunications needs. And yes, it was still a lot of work to start off with, but there was a new factor: I was doing this for me, and I was doing this for my customers. It was a night-and-day difference.

WHY ARE YOU HERE?
(AND WHERE ARE YOU TRYING TO GO?)

What is the driving factor for you to investigate franchising? When we look at getting people into franchising, answering that question is the first goal. What doesn't feel right in your life? Not enough time for yourself? Not enough time for the family? Is your corporate job just not doing it for you?

The main theme here is, "What are you really looking to accomplish?" or "What is your goal?"

Perhaps you don't have any issues. You might be doing great right now, and maybe you have no problems. If that's the case, you probably want to do better. A lot of my people are doing great already. In all cases, it's important to look at where you've been, what you're accomplishing, and what goals you want to set for yourself.

The next question we ask essentially flows from the first: What do you consider wealth? Is it simply more money? Is it more time for yourself? More time for your family? Is there something you want that requires more of your time or more of your money?

If you're in the corporate world, you might want extra income on the side to increase your options. You might enjoy having something so that you can step away from your job now and again. Or perhaps you don't like that corporate job at all and it's time to just leave it (like I did). When you reach that point, it is clearly time to move on.

You might be approaching retirement, but maybe you don't have quite enough to make that happen. As you ponder the possibilities, perhaps diversifying your stock options doesn't seem to be the answer. If this is your situation, wealth is most likely found in security.

Something has led you to this point. You are now thinking about getting into a business—particularly a franchise business. And if you're doing great already and you just want to do better overall, we can work with that as well. As I said before, quite a few of the people I've worked with were doing just fine running their own businesses—but investing in the stock market never seemed to cut it for them, so they wanted another form of investment. Now they've added a new line of investment to the equation, and it's only been a plus in their busy lives.

No matter the details, you're looking into a business that will be the solution to your problem—or the means to the ends you are looking to achieve. You don't want to spend all those hours working at a job with nothing to show for it at the end of the day except a paycheck and maybe some form of a 401(k) retirement plan. You want something to build up, something that you can continue having a manager run while you reap the benefits. You might even be looking for a business you can sell when you're done with it.

So, where are you going? As you spend time thinking about your ultimate goals, where do you find the next great investment? Do you look through the trade magazines to see which companies are doing well? Have you come up with your own idea? In Chapter 2, we'll go over this together.

FREEDOM (MY "ONE FRANCHISE AWAY")

So, there I was, just laid off. I had worked for the corporate world for thirty-something years. For a portion of that time, I determined that, yes, I could run a business on the side while I kept my corporate job. That was doable. As I shared above, I invested in a dry-cleaning business, but in the end "doable" wasn't the answer. My corporate job was just not cutting it for me. I knew this. Eventually, my employers knew it too.

Obviously, getting laid off is a blow. I had made it through many, many layoffs. In our industry, people were getting laid off all the time. When it was my turn, I was just like, "Oh my God. What am I going to do?" For most people, I think it can feel like the end of the world. But amazingly enough, it wasn't that way for me. I was almost jumping for joy. I was so excited that I was put into a position where I needed to go make a decision. *Do I go back and work in the corporate world? Do I find yet another job? Or do I commit to a new direction and get my own business?*

Ultimately, I knew, "Well, it's now or never." I mean, I found myself in a position where there was opportunity. They gave me severance pay, so I was good for about a year or so, plus I had some money that I'd saved up. As I thought about my options, I knew that I could not create the next best thing. I wouldn't be inventing something. I didn't have any ideas for a business of my own. In my head, that meant I couldn't be a true entrepreneur. However, from the books I read and my previous experiences, I knew that franchising was an option.

What next? I went and I looked for franchises. Of course, I found terrible options and good options. I eventually found the aforementioned telecommunications consulting franchise, but I'll share more on that later. Nonetheless, let me tell you, there was nothing more fulfilling than going out there and doing something for myself. It was so much better for me than having to get up and go to my job, working set hours every day.

This was the better path. Franchises have a business model for you. They've got the procedures and policies in place. You just step in, and you follow those policies and procedures. While your success is not guaranteed, it's much better than if you were to do it all by yourself. Ultimately, you have a partner in your success. As I realized all of this, I thought, *Boy, that is exactly what I need. I need a mentor. I need somebody who's going to show me how to do these things. I can follow policies and procedures. I can do this.*

I just needed a little help, and it sounded like franchising would provide that. When I got into my franchise, that was exactly how it went. When I visited with the team, they basically mapped it all out for me: "This is what we're going to do ... [step one, step two, step three, step four, and so on]." Ultimately, I just thought that this was just a really good sign. *All right, these folks have got it down. This is awesome. It's exactly what I'm looking for. I've got that mentor. I've got that help, those policies, the procedures, that step-by-step of how to do everything.*

I didn't need to create something by myself and yet it was still my business to run. I could do it at my own pace, my own speed, and my own time. I didn't answer to anybody but myself and, to a small extent, the franchise—but they're just there to help, because they want you to be successful. I couldn't help but feel relieved.

I'll share more about "Discovery Day," when you go out and meet the franchise team in person at their offices, later in the book. That occasion encouraged me to sign a franchise agreement. I won't lie to you: I woke up screaming—just one night, though. I couldn't stop myself from wondering what I was getting myself into. I knew it was what I wanted for myself; it was just that not knowing what exactly was ahead of me made me nervous. Aside from that, a burden was lifting. The need to go to a job day in and day out was gone. Moving forward, my success was entirely up to me and, after that one night, it was smooth sailing.

Once I was running my franchise, I was excited to get up in the morning and go out there and talk to businesspeople. Honestly, it didn't even matter to me how many hours I worked because it really wasn't working; it was just plain pure fun. Still, I had control of my schedule. Also, I was able to essentially not have an office that I had to go to every day, which was also a major factor for me.

In the end, it turned out that I wanted to be in business for myself. I didn't want to be limited by a location or an office, and I wanted to make my own schedule. These are exactly the factors that we talk to you about when it comes to getting into a franchise. What do you want to look at? Do you want schedule flexibility? Do you like going to an office every day? Or do you want to work wherever you want? Will your work life be the same or different than what you have now? No matter what, you'll be in business for yourself.

In Chapter 2, we'll determine what that business needs to be. Freedom is around the corner. You just need to choose it.

CHOOSING THE RIGHT FRANCHISE

In our first chapter, we realized that freedom is just a franchise away. Now, how do we find the right franchise? What are the steps that we take? What are all the mistakes to avoid? What are our options to consider?

When I figured out that my freedom was just a franchise away and that franchising was right for me, it was time to figure out which franchise was right for me. I had no idea where to start, so like everybody else I became click-happy. I went on Google and started searching on "franchises." This caused me to start getting all sorts of different calls from people. Every time you click and ask for information about a franchise, you will have people calling you up because you emailed and sent your information. How do we avoid that?

Let's take a look at Paula. I received her inquiry about franchising on Christmas Eve. I thought if she was out looking for such things in the middle of a holiday, she was really looking to make a big change in her life come the new year. As we communicated, I found her to be very interesting.

Paula was an IT staffer who had recently moved. Unfortunately, she discovered that in Oklahoma, corporations didn't pay as much for IT as she'd been getting over on the East Coast. She couldn't seem to find any corporate jobs that would pay her what she felt she was worth. As she looked to the future, she was very much realizing she would not be where she wanted to be upon retirement.

Paula enjoyed working and interacting with others. She enjoyed building teams and doing data analysis. After serving our country in the armed forces, she'd earned an engineering degree. Ultimately, she enjoyed working with computers, but that road seemed to be reaching a dead end. Initially, she made it clear to me that she was looking for an IT franchise where she could get paid as much as she had been making on the East Coast. She was hoping I could find her something that required the lowest possible investment, so she could use her own cash.

Paula was not aware of the funding options available to her and had actually dismissed funding altogether at first. I knew I could help her, but I also knew that the end result might not be what she had in mind—it could be even better. In this chapter, we'll go through what we did for Paula—as well as my own experience, the mistakes I made, and how I helped Paula avoid these same mistakes. Let's start with a few of my initial mishaps as I began my journey.

SEVEN FRANCHISING MISTAKES

1. *Not understanding the business/industry before getting started*

2. *Not figuring out how much the franchise costs (What is the investment level?)*

3. *Just because it's hot doesn't necessarily mean it's good for you*

4. *Thinking you'll be rich in a year or two ...*

5. *Not securing funding*

6. *Not talking to existing (or enough) franchisees*

7. *Not making use of free experts*

MISTAKE #1:
NOT UNDERSTANDING THE BUSINESS OR INDUSTRY BEFORE GETTING STARTED

Warren Buffett knows a lot about investing. He bypassed all the technology companies and stocks because he didn't understand the industry and refused to get involved in anything he didn't understand. That's what we help you avoid.

For me, starting out, that's one of the mistakes I made. I didn't understand all the different industries and what they encompass. I was clicking on all sorts of industries. What we help you do is understand the businesses, the industries, and the models. That way, you'll know what makes a particular franchise successful, how the margins work, and how likely it'll be profitable.

MISTAKE #2:
NOT FIGURING OUT HOW MUCH THE FRANCHISE COSTS (WHAT IS THE INVESTMENT LEVEL?)

On face value, many will say, "All right, so it takes $250,000 to invest in this franchise. That's how much I have, so I can afford that franchise." Well, not necessarily! It depends on the franchise itself.

You're going to need some working capital as well. This also depends entirely on the franchise that you're getting into. If you get into a franchise where you are the owner-operator, then you probably won't have a lot of overhead; you won't necessarily need a lot of working capital, except for maybe a good marketing budget. But say you're getting into a bricks-and-mortar type of franchise (like food service or automotive) which requires you to come up with a payroll and provide training, and you've got to build the concept. All of that requires not only investment but now you also need working capital.

We'll take a look at your budget and what kind of a budget it takes to get that franchise going. These are the sorts of things you'll need to know. I can provide you with information about how the business model works and what working capital you'll need, so you'll have a better, clearer understanding of what the total investment really is.

MISTAKE #3:
JUST BECAUSE IT'S HOT DOESN'T NECESSARILY MEAN IT'S GOOD FOR YOU

There are a lot of people who will come to me and ask, OK, what are the hot concepts out there? Remember, some hot concepts today may not be hot concepts tomorrow. We'll take a look at what it is you're really trying to accomplish. Are you wanting to tell everybody you have the hottest concept, or are you looking for a great investment that will pay your bills now and into the future—allowing you the lifestyle you want?

Keep in mind that not all hot concepts are bad. Each has pros and cons. Obviously, if it's a hot concept, you may make a lot of money quickly. As long as you can grow it and sell it within a certain amount of time, it may not be a bad idea. But these are some of the things I'll go over with you individually.

MISTAKE #4:
THINKING YOU'LL BE RICH IN A YEAR OR TWO

It will take time to build things up, but maybe if it's a hot concept, who knows? It could make a quick profit, but that is not something you should necessarily count on. I'm going to give you a realistic view of that when I'm taking you through the process of investigating a franchise.

In the process, you'll talk with many franchisees, and you'll find out just exactly how long it took them to get there, what it takes to get there, and how soon the money starts coming in. Keep in mind that the franchisees you will be speaking with were in your shoes when they were investigating franchises. They know what questions you are likely to ask and why you're asking them—even the money questions.

MISTAKE #5:
NOT SECURING FUNDING

Yes, there's always funding available. Many people are still fearful of funding because of the perceived risks. The investors I work with really do not like using their own money. They always want to use other people's money to fund their businesses, and there are many different ways of funding businesses. So, don't be afraid of looking into funding just to explore the options that are available to you.

Franchises are generally very easy to fund because they have proven track records. And we have people who fund franchises all the time and they will give you the information you need to decide if funding is right for you. In Chapter 5, we'll look a little more in-depth into the different types of funding that are available for franchises.

MISTAKE #6 (PART 1):
NOT TALKING TO EXISTING FRANCHISEES

No matter what, you'll want to get on the phone with an existing franchisee. This will give you a couple of things: (1) real-world information on how the franchise operates on a daily basis, and (2) a friend who will help you succeed.

The franchisors are going to be there to help you be successful. That's one of the things they provide with the franchise fee and with the ongoing royalties. They're all about being your mentor and making certain you succeed. We'll go over how the franchise fees and royalties work in Chapter 3.

Remember, the other franchisees want to you to succeed as well. The more the franchise name gets out there and the more people know about it, the faster it grows. That's win-win all around.

MISTAKE #6 (PART 2):
NOT TALKING TO ENOUGH EXISTING FRANCHISEES

That's right. I said it again because it's that important: you'll want to talk to as many as it takes for you to get a good feel for that business. Not only are you getting a good feel, but you're also making friends along the way.

The franchise's role is to help you be successful. Now, as you're talking to franchisees, you're making friends, and these people are going to be people you'll call upon to help you out when you're getting started, as well as the franchise. You'll want to talk to as many of them as it takes for you to start hearing the same thing over and over again. That way you'll know, once you get to that point, that you have probably talked to enough of them.

Keep in mind that not everybody is equal. A lot of money to some people is not a lot to others. Some people may be happy as can be making a hundred thousand dollars a year, and some people may not. A hundred thousand (or less) may be all they need, and they won't want to put any more hours into it.

You may talk to another franchisee who says, "Well, yeah. I'm doing a million dollars a year. This is awesome. This is how I do it." If you want to be one of the top people, then you'll want to get on the phone with the franchisees who are making the most money. Find out what it is they do on a daily basis and picture yourself doing that.

If you can picture yourself doing the actions of a top performer, you're probably on the right track to becoming one of them yourself. If you cannot picture yourself doing that, then you've got two options: (1) we'll find you another franchise to look at, or (2) you hire somebody to do it for you. Either way, always talk and listen to franchisees.

MISTAKE #7:
NOT MAKING USE OF FREE EXPERTS

There are lots of experts out there. We have experts in funding. We have attorney experts. Look up the SCORE chapter in your area (SCORE.org). The members are all, or have been, businesspeople. These are the business mentors you can get a hold of.

I talked to a few different SCORE people when I was looking into getting a franchise myself. They are some of the greatest people around. They have all been in business for quite some time. They gave me a lot of great insights into what I should look for in a business and whether the business would be successful in the environment we're in now. So, always make use of as many free experts as possible.

> For more information on these seven mistakes,
> go to franchisemaven.com.

I made sure that Paula did not make these mistakes. I made certain that she understood the business and industries that she was looking at. I made certain that she had capital. We looked at different franchises, not just the ones that were fashionable. She knew it would take some time; she wouldn't necessarily be rich in a year or two. We looked at funding options. She spoke with existing franchisees from the different franchises she was investigating, and then she talked to experts as well.

TYPES OF FRANCHISES

There are many types of franchises to get into. One of the things that I will send you to begin with is the franchise business matrix. You can review it yourself at franchisemaven.com and look at the business matrix there.

We'll review the business matrix together. Within that main business matrix, we have four basic categories:

QUADRANT A: *Simple Retail Businesses*

QUADRANT B: *Sophisticated Retail Businesses*

QUADRANT C: *Business-to-Consumer*

QUADRANT D: *Business-to-Business*

WHERE DO YOU SEE YOURSELF?

QUADRANT A: *Simple Retail Businesses*
People need it and come to you. This includes your basic restaurants, Great Clips, fitness franchises, that sort of thing—simple, easy businesses to get into.

QUADRANT B: *Sophisticated Retail Businesses*
You provide a skilled service that people may need. We're looking at something where you're going to have more skilled employees who have certain backgrounds. These are businesses like Meineke, Midas, AAMCO, MAACO, urgent care, and weight-loss clinics where they may need some certification for what they do—things the general

public needs every day but that require a bit more licensing and back-ground to do.

One pro of Quadrants A and B is that they're easily scalable. When you're looking at bricks-and-mortar types of businesses, if you open one, you can open another. If you can run two, then you could probably run ten. I know one person who is picking up his fiftieth salon. He just picked up another pack of twenty-eight because he's looking to get a hundred.

The cons are that they can be more of an investment. Bricks-and-mortar locations carry build-out and fixed costs. You're going to need a lot of people. You or your manager will be doing a lot of hiring on a regular basis.

In Quadrants C and D, we're looking at service businesses. With service businesses, your clients do not necessarily know you exist until they need you.

QUADRANT C: *Business-to-Consumer*
For elder care, childcare, or property services; you don't necessarily need a storefront.

QUADRANT D: *Business-to-Business*
Making your back office somebody's front office. Anything that a business needs, there is probably a franchise to provide it.

A lot of these businesses don't have name recognition—meaning you most likely haven't heard of them. The Belfor Group is a company that does restoration services. Most likely, you're only aware of them if you've had water, smoke, or fire damage—Paul Davis Restoration is the same way. The Belfor Group is huge. They did half of the cleanup after Hurricane Katrina, but few people would have heard about them. Paul Davis Restoration is nearly the same in size—they are found in most of the United States.

The pros: It takes a lot less capital to get service businesses started. You may be providing most of the labor initially, but you don't have to—you can hire people to do that for you. It's not as capital-intensive to scale this up.

The cons: You're going to be the one out there selling yourself. You're going out there and getting in front of people so they can know, like, and trust you, so that they want to work with you. You don't necessarily have to do that yourself. If you want to, you can hire people to go out and do the sales and do the work for you as well. But if you want to start it yourself, you're generally going to be the one out there doing it.

As we spend time going over Quadrants A to D, one of the things we'll be asking you is, where do you see yourself in those? Some people have specific areas in mind, and others are open. We'll go over that together. Take advantage of the local SCORE team. They will help you out—I know they helped me out when I was looking.

PAUSE
(FIGURE IT OUT, GREG!)

As I was going through the quadrants and looking at different franchises, I got a call from a franchise consultant. At the time, I had no idea that there were franchise consultants out there (and now I am one). There are a lot of people who don't know what a franchise consultant is, which means they really don't know what we do.

I found a couple of consultants who were out there to help me, which was really nice. They said, "Put everything on hold for a minute." So, I did. I started working with them and they took me down that path of figuring out:

- What am I really looking for in life?

- What am I looking to accomplish?

- Am I looking for an investment?

- Am I looking for a purpose in life and an investment, or just a purpose in life?

I found that working with them really made me think, which was well worth the time. I also found that franchise consultants don't charge anything. The franchisors we work with pay us a referral fee if you decide to invest in a franchise we introduce you to. We've got to be good at what we do when we put you in front of a franchise, and it's got to be the right franchise for you—one that you feel good about, you want to get involved with, and you want to invest in. Then, and only then, do we get paid.

We found a telecommunications consulting franchise that was a great fit for me. I got to work from home. I'd go out and visit with my clients on a regular basis. I could do any kind of schedule that I wanted to do. I found cost savings for them as clients in the telecommunications world, which was great, and I got to talk with all sorts of wonderful, interesting people.

I did the telecommunications franchise for a couple of years. Ultimately though, I chose the path of a franchise consultant. We help you understand the business, the business model, and the opportunity. We're going to put you on the phone with the franchise development people, rather than just the sales folks. We're going to put you on the phone with franchisees. We're going to make certain that when you get on the phone, we're going to have questions for you, for the franchisor, and for the franchisee.

As I was getting started, the thing I didn't know was, "What do I ask them? Well, what am I looking for? How do I delve deep into that franchise?"

The franchise consultants will give you the list of questions to ask franchisors and franchisees. You'll obviously have your list—but they will have a list for you as well. I will have this for you. These will be in-depth questions to ask the franchisors and the franchisees about the business.

That's what I did with Paula as well. I made certain Paula understood what the franchises would require, and we looked at the IT businesses that initially held her interest. However, we also looked further into Paula's background, and that led to quite the surprise (more on this shortly).

We discussed the reality of funding, and I introduced Paula to our funding experts. With their guidance she was able to determine that, with the right franchise, a loan would work for her. Knowing this was available opened her mind to new possibilities she had disregarded before. Outside of IT, Paula did not know of the many different industries that might be a better fit. Once we started going over the various franchises in the various industries, it was like a light turning on inside her.

Believe it or not, Paula is no longer an IT professional! Paula is now running a mechanic shop, because we found out she loved cars. We got her out of the IT business and into an automotive service station franchise. She's very happy doing what she always enjoyed as a hobby. While she isn't doing any restoration or repair work herself, she has always enjoyed working with cars and now she has a business that does just that.

And the positive developments didn't end there! The auto franchise that she joined also allowed her the time to explore doing more work in the IT field as an independent consultant. I never really asked Paula how much she's making as a franchisee in the auto service industry or how it compares to how much she was making in the IT services business. I never needed to. She enjoys it so much that the topic of money never seems to come up.

Our work with Paula represents our most desirable result. Without our guidance, she may have settled for more of the same old, same old. Instead, she found a way to keep the best of both worlds—tech and automotive, her old love. There's no beating that.

Franchising is a great plan for building wealth—the greatest, as I'll explain in the next chapter. If you're curious what we can do for you, please visit franchisemaven.com. Check out our resources on the seven mistakes and review the business matrix. You can also see about using a franchise consultant. Always, whenever you have questions, don't hesitate to call, email, or text me at any time at franchisemaven.com.

CHAPTER 3

THE GREATEST PLAN FOR BUILDING WEALTH

In our last chapter, you learned how I went about looking to get into a franchise, what mistakes I made, and how I help my clients avoid them. We went over Paula's story and how I helped her avoid those mistakes. We also went over the franchise business matrix and the different types of franchise businesses that you can get into. And then I addressed the importance of using a good franchise consultant.

If you haven't already, for further information you can check out the seven mistakes, the business matrix, and using a franchise consultant on franchisemaven.com. Now that we know what to look for and what to avoid, along with the options available, it's time for the plan.

Kat came to me looking to build an empire. Kat came to the United States from India twenty years ago as an engineering and computer consultant. He is passionate about life and helping others, building win-win relationships in the way he could acquire cash flowing apartment buildings and businesses.

With a master's degree in management and engineering, he was the CEO and IT director of a business that kept him busy most of the time— but it wasn't enough. On his present course he was not getting to where he wanted to be as quickly as he had hoped. He wanted to know what he could do to build his empire with multiple units (this actually touches on the different levels of franchising: the single unit, the area developer, and the master franchise).

Until speaking with me, he had been dismissing franchise ownership as an option for wealth creation. That meant he was unaware of how area developer franchising worked and did not know it could be a vehicle to get him to his ultimate goals. As he had the cash available, he wouldn't need any funding—which meant he could get started right away. He was driven toward enabling his ability to continue helping others, and we were ready to help him achieve that. But first he needed a plan—the greatest plan of all.

NO PROMISES

Before we go through the various franchise options available for you, I need to address something very important. Quite often people will ask me, "How much can I make?" The Federal Trade Commission restricts what we can say about what you can make.

This is because long, long ago in a land far, far away, the franchise salespeople would say, "If you get this franchise, you can make _____ amount of money." Some people did, some people did not. And those who did not were not too happy, to say the least, resulting in a lot of lawsuits that caused the Federal Trade Commission to step in.

We don't have exact information on how much franchisees make, and no franchise consultant does. Only the franchise collects that information and, as such, only they can tell. And they can really only tell if they have that information in their franchise disclosure documents.

SINGLE UNIT, AREA DEVELOPER, OR MASTER FRANCHISE

Most people start off with a single unit of a franchise. You buy one unit and, depending on the franchise, it will have a territory. Probably 90 percent or more of our franchises have a particular delineated territory.

Territory size will depend on the franchise itself. If it's a bricks-and-mortar-type franchise, the territory is generally going to have a radius of a mile, in which the franchisee has exclusive rights, and the franchisor will not grant anyone else a franchise. You won't have to compete with another of the same franchise.

If it's a service industry type of franchise, the territory size of the franchise that you get into is determined by the population density of the customers who will use your services—instead of the territory being marked geographically, the territory is measured by the projected population density, for individual users or businesses.

For a single-unit franchise, you'd most likely be looking at 100,000 to 200,000 people with a household income of $100,000. Just know that you need to make sure they have the disposable income available. This is one of the items we will be reviewing together on our calls.

If you want to start out with something bigger, you can do an area-developer franchise. With an area-developer franchise, you'll buy more than one territory at a reduced cost (as Kat was trying to build an empire, this was what caught his interest). You can do this a single unit at a time, but someone else might pick up the territory adjacent to you and then you can't build there. Instead, what you can do is ask for an area-developer license.

At this point in time, you feel really good about the franchise. You believe in it. You know that these are the types of people you want to work with. You know this concept is going to take off because we've gathered the information for you to make an informed decision.

Let's say you buy ten territories. You will have a plan for how you're going to build those out. You may do one the first year, two the second year, three the third year, and so on—this is going to vary by franchise. You'll need a plan for building out the area, but you'll be able to take over a whole city. You're building every single unit. You're paying for them, staffing them, operating them, and incurring all the costs and all the profits minus the royalties—that is an area developer.

Similar to that is a master franchise. A master franchise is where you are taking over an entire area. That can involve anywhere from five to ten or twenty units or more—depending on the population density of your city and how many territories the franchise calculates will fit in that area. As a master franchiser, you're more like the right arm of the actual franchise. The franchise is going to teach you how to train others and how to be a franchisee. You can have an entire city or even a whole state, for that matter—it depends on how much you want to invest.

You build out your pilot and then you will train new franchisees. You then sell your territories within your master franchise agreement. When you sell your territories, you receive about 50 percent of that franchise fee (this varies by franchise). As your new franchisee grows, you share in the royalties, which are generally between 5 and 10 percent. As an area developer, you are building out and putting your money into a new territory. However, as a master franchisor, you have someone else do it. While you're not getting all the profits from it, neither are you investing all the money to build out that unit as a master.

Master franchising is one of the better ways to build an empire with less work because you're not running each franchise individually. As a master franchisor, you are an entrepreneur. You're purchasing the rights to a larger territory, then helping new franchisees open their locations in your exclusive territory, following an agreed-upon schedule. Generally, you would hire a manager to run your pilot unit—you wouldn't do that yourself because you're going to be spending your time developing new franchisees and selling new territories.

INVESTMENT INVOLVED

This is the superior investment vehicle because of the return-on-investment (ROI) potential. You receive revenues from multiple streams: revenue from your pilot unit itself, from the initial franchise fee, from each franchise that you have sold, and then from your ongoing royalty fees. If you have ten units, you've got royalties coming in from all of them. Once the units are developed, you're not doing anything except overseeing. The managers of those franchises are running them. You are not paying the rent for any franchised locations, and you don't have to run payroll for any of the franchise units because the franchisee is doing all that.

I have some charts that can give you a breakdown of the ROIs that are associated with master franchising. When you take a look at those illustrations, you can see that you can generate a pretty significant front-end revenue and help support the early-stage development of those businesses—help them increase sales, which means the percentage of royalties is going to go up. Keep in mind that the information I provide in these charts is just a simplified example of the start-up and operations of a master franchise business.

Investment costs themselves will vary depending on the nature of the franchise business. If you're looking at developing an area for a bricks-and-mortar type of franchise, it's going to be a little bit different. Nevertheless, you do have the opportunity for a very high return and to build a business that can not only provide a superior income stream but also create a source of long-term revenue. All of this can make a positive impact on your financial future—not just for you but for generations to come.

For the capable entrepreneur, investigating and operating a master developer business is viewed as an attractive investment, like the stock market or real estate. It remains under your control for the entire time. Keep in mind this difference between being a master franchisor versus an area developer.

As an area developer, you will invest in every single unit and you will get all of the returns, minus the royalties that you have to pay.

You are going to be investing your money in each one of those units and you will be operating them yourself.

For more discussion of the pros and cons, please visit my website franchisemaven.com.

With a master franchise, the good point is you're not going to be using all your money to invest in every single one of those units. Someone else will be investing money in your franchises, but that way you won't be getting all the proceeds. The profits will still provide a very good income stream, one that will stay with you for generations to come.

HORIZONTAL AND VERTICAL GROWTH

With both master and area developer franchising, there is horizontal growth. Vertical growth is another thing you can do with both master and developer franchising. What is vertical growth? Let's take home improvement services as an example. You own a home improvement and painting franchise, and you go into the home of clients who want you to paint their house. You look at the interior or exterior they want painted and you see there's a lot of things on the house that need to be repaired.

Now, you *could* just paint over the problems and leave all those things still broken. Does that sound like it's not a nice thing to do? You're likely right. What you'd probably do is tell the client it would be a good idea to fix some of those things first, before you paint over them. If you only own a painting franchise, then you could send them to someone else to get all the work done before you can paint. If you also own a home improvement or maintenance franchise, and you practice vertical growth, you could actually bring your own handyman, as well as your painting franchise. In this case, you would say, "OK, I'm going to send my handyman."

It goes the other way too. If you're a handyman, you go out and start fixing things. But maybe the home you're working on needs to be repainted, so you say, "Hey, I've got a painting company. After we get done with this, why don't we just repaint everything?" While you're there, if they don't have a maid service, you could ask, "Hey, why don't I just have my maid service come over to clean up afterward?"

You're doing marketing and advertising to one person for the two to four different services that you can provide to that client. Your marketing costs are a lot less because you're working with one client on one home with multiple things that can be done. That is vertical growth—franchises that have multiple different types of franchises within their group.

On my franchisemaven.com, I have a master development plan for you that you can go through with numbers from the charts that I refer to, with a bit of breakdown on the ROI. If you have any questions, I can be contacted through franchisemaven.com.

BUILDING AN EMPIRE

Beyond helping others, Kat had a very specific mission: to use his wealth and his relationships to provide affordable patient-centered healthcare with excellence in compassion, service, and outcome. We took a look at the plan with Kat. I suggested to him the master franchise route. Once we started going over the various levels—single unit, area developer, and master franchising—he saw that being an area developer would get him to where he wanted to be.

Kat wanted to operate every one of his single units, and he found managers as he built up each one. With every few franchises, he would not only have a manager in the franchise itself but a regional manager as well. He did that because he wanted the profits from each of those businesses. He didn't mind investing, building those out, and getting those done.

Toward the fulfillment of this purpose and mission, he is now acquiring large hospitals, medical centers, and manufacturers of medical products and devices, in part by using the money he's making on his franchises. He loves the plan and he loves fulfilling it! He has businesses in a couple of different areas, and his goal was to get one hundred of the same franchise because he loves his franchise. Right now, he has thirty-three in a couple of cities and is in the process of picking up forty-eight more in a couple of other cities where he has a presence. His dream of building an empire is coming true.

The next step is to review that master franchisor plan on franchisemaven. com. If you have any questions, there are plenty of ways to reach out to me on franchisemaven.com. Please don't hesitate to do so. In the next chapter, I'll share more about the investment levels of franchising, and the opportunities therein.

CHAPTER 4

INVESTMENT LEVELS

In our last chapter, we talked about the different levels of franchising: single, master, and area-developer franchises. We defined the pros and cons of each level. We also went through the experience of Kat, who is on his way to building an empire. In our next step, we will go into more detail about the different levels of franchises. Within single, master, and area-developer franchises, there are two types of business—bricks-and-mortar and service franchises—which we will go over.

One thing many people ask me is, "If I invest more money, will I get a higher return on the investments?" No, that is not necessarily true, which brings us to Patricia's story. Patricia was looking for a bricks-and-mortar franchise with her dad and pretty much their whole family. When they came to me, she was a director of marketing and sales with a political science degree. She really wanted to help her dad out (nice children give us dads something to do).

Initially, she had been looking into established franchises for sale, or as we refer to them, *resales*, so that's where we began our conversation. As we started looking into bricks-and-mortar resale franchises, Patricia realized this might not the best fit for her dad—or even herself. It turns out Patricia wanted eventually to walk away from her job. While she liked working with cross-functional teams, she didn't like the bureaucracy involved with the approval process. It had probably taken her about eight years to build up to the point where she was, and she was a little tired of it. She decided that she wanted something semi-absentee, so she could eventually step away from the job when she was ready financially. In her free time, Patricia enjoyed fitness and travel.

As we dug deeper into Patricia's interests outside work, we discussed fitness and travel. However, when we talked to her dad, we were able to establish that her father really liked fixing and working on things. Ultimately, Patricia just didn't want to be stuck in her job with absolutely no means to walk away from it whenever she needed—and being able to pursue this new opportunity with her family meant a lot to her. Her original instincts were focused on the simplicity of resale, semi-absentee, and bricks-and-mortar.

Now that we were on the same page with everybody—the family was excited about getting involved, especially with their dad—we were getting a better sense of what would work for them. First, I discovered that while Patricia had definitely researched franchises on her own, she made one of the seven mistakes from Chapter 1: she never really spoke or met with any franchisees. As soon as I understood that, I knew how to get everyone moving.

However, before I continue, let's take a look at specific franchise types, business opportunities, and levels of investment.

BRICKS-AND-MORTAR FRANCHISES (YOU BUILD IT AND THEY WILL COME)

When you're looking at a bricks-and-mortar franchise, you will want to look at franchises that have a real estate team that can find the real estate for you. Not only are they going to find the real estate for you, but you can also have them do the lease negotiation for you.

A great franchise system will not expect you to be the prime real estate person. They will expect you to be a good businessperson but not necessarily expect you to know where to find the right real estate.

You're going to be putting bricks-and-mortar franchises in A-plus real estate locations. People are going to drive by and see you, and they're going to come into your businesses. Of course, you will still be doing the marketing and advertising in your area, but it will be different from the type of marketing and advertising for the services industry.

McDonald's, Burger King, Taco Bell, Supercuts, Great Clips, Meineke, Maaco, and some of the computer repair places will be in bricks-and-mortar strip malls as well.

Once we get into the bricks-and-mortar and get that built, we will be looking at having an exclusive territory. Any franchise system will give you an exclusive territory, meaning you won't be competing with any other franchisees in the same franchise system. Generally speaking, you're going to be looking at a radius in terms of miles.

Bricks-and-mortar is obviously going to require the highest investment level, or at least one that is higher than for a service industry. You either have a complete build, or you're in a strip mall and you just need to refurbish the inside of the location that the franchise has picked out for you. Generally speaking, if you're looking at that it will require a total investment of $300,000 to $400,000 or more. That includes the franchise fee, getting it built, getting everybody trained, and getting the business running. Generally speaking, that's the cost you're looking at.

The franchises are all going to be looking for you to have a net worth of about $500,000, with about $100,000 of it liquid. They don't want you to run out of money before you get started. The loan companies will also be looking for something like that when you're starting a bricks-and-mortar franchise.

Different franchises will do different things with bricks-and-mortar, so with some bricks-and-mortar franchises you don't necessarily have to put it up completely brand new and refurbish the whole thing to make your franchise. There are a few franchisors who will actually buy out privately owned businesses and convert them into franchises.

Just because you're investing more in bricks-and-mortar, this does not necessarily mean that you are going to make more money. Some of the bricks-and-mortar franchises bring in less than a six-figure income per year, while some in the service industry can put you in the six-figure income range.

They are, however, very simple to operate. You have somebody else run them, build up a few of them, pay your managers good money, and get a regional manager and then you might be bringing in under a six-figure income per location a year straight to your pocket. Some of our bricks-and-mortar franchises actually bring in a multiple-six-figure-a-year income. So, it varies, but investing more doesn't necessarily bring in more money. (Disclaimer: This is not an earnings claim, just an example that a bigger investment does not necessarily equate to more earnings. For more information on earning, see Chapter 7 and the franchise disclosure document.)

SERVICE FRANCHISES

Within the service industry, your clients do not necessarily know you exist until they need you. You'll need a good franchise system that will drive people to you when the need arises. Think of things like restoration services for fire, water, and smoke damage. When people have a problem at their house or business, you want your franchise to be the one that pops up first. You want a good franchise system that will drive people to you when they need you. This concept also refers to senior care, placing seniors into facilities, tutoring, restoration services, home improvement services, kitchen remodel, garage organization, pest control, roofing, irrigation systems, insulation systems, and business services.

Now, with the service industry, you're looking at an investment of about $150,000. After you get it up and running, there is a potential for a good six-figure income, depending on the franchise (not an earnings claim). The franchise disclosure documents (FDDs) will give you insight into the potential income; follow that up and verify it by speaking to franchisees (more on FDDs in Chapter 7).

What you're going to look for with the services industry is that the franchise will drive people to you when the need arises. One of the things you may need is a call center. People will look you up online and make a call. Now, if you don't want to be handling those calls all the time, there are various levels of call centers that these franchises will have in place. You'll want a system that takes the calls and schedules appointments for you. They have your scheduler, they know when you're available, and they schedule the appointments. Some will even give estimates over the phone to your clients.

Look for the various levels of call centers; some will do more than others. Some of the franchises in the services industry will also produce leads for you—leads being customers. That's something to look into—how they provide leads for you.

All good franchises in the services industry will have everything in place for you: where to find people—not only your clients and your customers—and how to market to them and network. You're also going to need workers. In some franchises you can do everything yourself, but there are others that may provide people to do things for you, such as pest control and remodeling. In any case, you'll still want a system that's going to show you how to do that.

For instance, in the senior-care industry, you're going to be employing a lot of caregivers. How do you find those caregivers? Where do you look? What should you ask? You'll want a good franchise system that's going to have all that in place for you so you're never guessing or wondering, "OK, what do I do next?" You don't want to be in that position. You want to have a clear plan for the franchise, with steps to follow.

Territory size in the services industry is going to be a little bit different. You're targeting consumers, so you're going to be looking at the density of the consumer population and this can range from 100,000 to 300,000 people. The actual physical size of your territory, where no other franchisee will be allowed, will vary depending on your population density.

You should also be looking at household income—specifically disposable income. So, when you're looking at services like home improvement, pest control, or tutoring, generally speaking you should be looking for 100,000 to 300,000 people who each have disposable income of about $100,000 or more.

Within the services industry there's a type that uses a small office and another that allows you to work from home. There are franchises that require you to go out and call upon your clients. They won't ever come to your office. You can go to them and basically work from home. Some of the business-to-business franchises are like that too.

With the services industry, your total investment will be on the lower end—normally about $150,000 if you need an office. The $150,000 will get you a small office, a lease, computers, desks, and whatever else you need to get that business going. Working from home generally needs an investment of about $100,000. No outside office would be needed, so this is eliminated from the cost.

Again, with a bricks-and-mortar franchise, if you build it, they will come. Again, in the services industry your clients don't necessarily know you exist until they need you. As you consider these alternatives, you and I will go through the process of determining which one will be right for you.

BUSINESS OPPORTUNITIES

In addition to franchises, you'll also find what we call business opportunities. These opportunities are a little bit different from franchises in that you don't necessarily need to pay a franchise fee and you don't have ongoing royalties. If you're looking to get involved, we usually have at least a couple that we can present to you.

In terms of expectations, this avenue is similar to owning franchises. The business opportunities still have benefits like great support systems and training. Rather than franchise fees, startup costs are more focused on acquiring the initial equipment you need; sometimes you can buy it directly from the opportunity source, but this is not a necessity.

A big advantage with business opportunities is that you'll have a little bit more leeway in running the business. For example, you aren't limited to the business name like you are with franchising—you can set yourself up with whatever name you like! You also won't necessarily be restricted by territory, as you are with a franchise system.

Back to royalties: something you'll want to keep in mind is ensuring you understand how the business opportunity stays in business. That's part of what we consider when we present anything we find to you. We all want to be sure the opportunity providers can continue supporting and training you. It's important to consider how they're getting things done on their end.

As an example, I'll share some insight regarding one of the sign companies that we work with. To get started, you can either buy all the necessary equipment needed to make all signs, or you can work with their vendors, who can help you build the signs. The sign company business opportunity will start you off with a basic package which you will purchase from it. To make signs that you do not have the equipment for, the sign company will provide vendors who are part of the organization. These vendors pay a fee to be part of the organization, and that is one of the ways the sign company makes money to stay in business. It makes a lot of money that way, and you can also buy supplies from that particular sign company, which is another way it makes money.

As I said, you need to assess the ways the business opportunities make money and stay in business, so that you don't find yourself doing it completely alone down the line. There are some great options to consider, especially if you're looking for some of the good things that go with franchises, such as support and training, but with a little more freedom. Overall, I find that it's good to at least consider business opportunities so you can have something to compare to the franchises we present you.

Another difference is that business opportunities don't involve franchise disclosure documents (more on FDDs in Chapter 7). On first impression, this might sound like a positive to you. Let's dig a little deeper. When you're looking into a franchise, lists of current and previous franchisees must by law be made available to you. With a business opportunity, you won't have that resource. That means you won't be able to call those people to see what their experiences were or continue to be.

Those FDD lists come with contact information and names. With a business opportunity, you'll be reliant on only the information they choose to provide, which makes for a challenge. You'd need to be able to build trust based on whatever they give you. Visibility is a big advantage with franchises as it will certainly help you determine the best fit—rather than moving forward partially blind. You really have to believe in the business opportunity and have confidence that they will be transparent with you by providing the necessary information.

This brings me back to territory. Returning to the example of a sign company, one would think that they would put good effort into avoiding sales cannibalization, in which they have too many people serving their target demographic in one area. However, they aren't required to run things that way, and you'll only be able to confirm the details based on what they tell you.

The business opportunities we work with run things well. We have the sign business that I've mentioned, and they've been at it for about thirty years. It's just good to know that there's another option to consider. No matter which way you go, you should believe in the company you're signing with. For some of my clients, it really is enough to hear "no royalties" for them to go straight to a business opportunity I'm presenting. Some of them do this, and they do great.

There are good business opportunities out there, and we can direct you to the ones we've had success with over the years. In terms of investing, the requirements can be pretty much the same as for franchises. Some of the service industries can involve $50,000 to $100,000. Some of the small office types can run to around $200,000.

RELATABLE SERVICE

Let's return to Patricia's story. She really wanted her family, especially her dad, involved in whatever option she chose. After her initial thoughts about resale bricks-and-mortar, I asked what she was really trying to accomplish, what her goals and criteria were. This led to new discussions on other interests she had outside of resale bricks-and-mortar opportunities and how they would fit into her goals and criteria. It eventually came up that neither she nor her dad had really spoken to any franchisee while they did their research. That meant they were missing out on much-needed perspectives.

I suggested that to get the ball rolling, Patricia and her family should actually communicate with current and previous franchisees (this is essential, and I can't stress that enough). This would give them a chance to hear their experiences, learn the background of their situations, and generally find out how things work on a regular basis. At first, Patricia's response was, "Well, I don't want to waste anybody's time, especially my own."

To this I asked, "Since when is learning a waste of time?"

She laughed and agreed with me.

Knowing that Patricia's dad would be heavily involved, especially while Patricia was still working, we switched our focus from bricks-and-mortar to service franchises. We found some interesting handyman options—fixing things, tinkering, and the like—and Patricia's family took my advice on meeting with people. These other franchisees were completely honest with them as to what could be expected in terms of both daily activities and how much they could expect to make. Patricia could then visualize what she could work with and where she could win.

Eventually, they went out and visited franchises. They actually made a lot of good friends along the way, enjoyed their time, and related to everyone. This was especially useful for her dad, who would really be running the business while Patricia worked in the background.

When you talk to the franchisees, make sure you can relate to what they do if you're going to be directly involved in it—especially if you're the one working in the business on a daily basis, not in a semi-absentee way. Get in front of franchisees, talk to them, find out what they do, and picture yourself doing it. Patricia's dad did this and ended up going bowling with a group from one particular franchise. He had a great time and enjoyed connecting with everyone he met. He felt like he was one of them.

Patricia and her family went ahead and chose their handyman franchise. In the end, we were able to get them a Small Business Administration (SBA) loan (more on this in the next chapter). This business remained a family affair, with her dad being *in* the business while Patricia worked *on* it. They really had a sense of freedom as they built their business and spent more time together as a family. And that freedom spread. Patricia was able to step away from her other job completely and focus on their new adventure.

Let's recap. When Patricia first came to me, her expectation was for a bricks-and-mortar resale franchise. Please note, ones like these require more investment as resale can add expenses to the equation. Overall, needing multiple locations, purchasing or leasing equipment needed inside the building, and the earnings that they would need to be paying out as well, all meant they would need to invest $250,000 to $300,000 or so. When they chose the handyman franchise, this brought their required investment down to around $150,000.

They had been considering a hair salon when they were still considering bricks-and-mortar franchises. Ultimately, as her dad was the one working *in* the business, that didn't feel like the best fit. Their final decision led to something they could both enjoy building and tinkering with together. Adding to the benefit of family time, they were able to accomplish this with a much smaller investment.

To answer the question from the beginning of the chapter, a larger investment doesn't necessarily mean a higher payout. For Patricia and her dad, there were so many other elements worth considering that went beyond the money involved. Together, they choose a path to freedom that worked best for them, and that result is priceless.

In the next chapter, now that we've covered the levels of investment, let's take a deeper look into financing the investment. As I shared previously, Patricia went with an SBA loan, but that's not the only option. The freedom of franchising has a cost, but that doesn't make it impossible. More on this in Chapter 5.

CHAPTER 5

FINANCING OPTIONS

In the last chapter, we talked about two different levels of franchises: bricks-and-mortar and service (as well as business opportunities). Whichever direction you choose, the next thing to figure out is how you are going to pay for it. There are many different financing and funding options out there. Keep in mind I am not an expert in financing; I have people for that. When the time is right, I will introduce you to them.

There was a moment when I almost went bankrupt. OK, it was not quite that bad, but I did not have the cash on hand to invest in a franchise. I had to look for another way to fund my plan, so I ended up using my 401(k) account to do it (we'll go over that shortly). Ten years later, I have about ten times the amount I started with, which for me made it a good thing to do. This is not for everybody. There are a lot of people who like to put that money in reserves and never touch it until it is time to retire.

Let's take a look at the various funding options available:

- 401(k) rollover
- Small Business Administration (SBA) loans
- Unsecured and blended loans

401(K) ROLLOVER

You've got the 401(k) business financing. If you don't want to go into debt and you've recently left your job, you have your 401(k) money. If you're working a new job, you've got a 401(k), but you cannot use it all for funding your business. So here, we're talking about using a 401(k) plan from the previous job and previous employer.

Well, what do you do with that? You convert it into a self-directed 401(k) plan. With a self-directed 401(k) plan, you now have money to use if you so desire (within IRS guidelines, of course). Keep in mind that I had left my job, so I had that 401(k) money sitting there. Once you have a self-directed 401(k) plan, you can buy stock in any business you want. You can buy stock in a C corporation, and the C corporation you're going to buy stock in is your C corporation.

The first thing that my people, my funding folks, help you with is to create that C corporation. My corporation was called Mohr, Inc. (yeah, pretty original, huh?) Then I was able to issue stocks from Mohr, Inc. Again, our funding people will arrange all of this for you, so you don't have to. They will walk you through it all.

You're going to need a C corporation so that stocks can be issued. You will have a checking account in your C corporation's name. You'll then buy stock in your C corporation using your self-directed 401(k) plan. You take that money from your 401(k) plan, and you transfer it over to your C corporation checking account, which can then issue you stock certificates.

I had stock certificates. I wrote them all out, and I made it all legal. I had one binder for everything. Our people will walk you through all that. It's a very simple process that sounds complicated but really isn't when you have the right people helping you out.

You bought stock in your corporation. You've transferred the money from your 401(k) plan into your C corporation checking account. Now your 401(k) plan has stock in your C corporation. This was all done with IRS compliance. Generally speaking, you're looking at a charge of around $5,000 to do the whole thing. You're going to pay monthly fees for the funding company that creates your 401(k) plan to monitor accounts and make certain that you stay within the IRS guidelines (generally speaking, this will cost $120 to $150 a month). Then, once a year, you'll have the stock valuation done on that corporation as well.

This is what I felt was a better way to go without going into debt. I did not want to go into debt or use other people's money. I just wanted to use what I had to do it. Along the way, you now have your own business, so you start putting money back into your 401(k) plan. There are lots of benefits, tax benefits, to going that route. You will, of course, have to pay corporation tax and then, when you take the money out, you will have to pay payroll tax.

It's a good thing to go over this with your accountant. You might have to get together with the funding people to whom I will introduce you to do the 401(k) rollover plan and schedule a meeting with your CPA or your financial advisor. The 401(k) funding folks will do that (they did for me). They can go over all the details with you. This is a way that not a lot of people know about to invest in a business, and you don't go into debt when you invest in your business.

One of the things about the 401(k) plan is that it usually takes about three weeks to arrange all the funding, which is relatively quick. You should have at least $40,000 in your plan to make it worthwhile. You need to take out $5,000 for the fees and ongoing fees. You can work with a 401(k), IRA, 403B, TSB, and so on. You also must be an employee of the business that you are operating.

SMALL BUSINESS ADMINISTRATION (SBA) LOANS

Another way to obtain financing is with Small Business Administration loans. The information I outline here is always subject to change, but with SBA loans you can go a few different routes:

1. Express loan
2. Term loan
3. Portfolio loan

You can get what they call an express loan, which has the benefits of a traditional SBA loan but without the personal collateral requirements. You can access up to $150,000. With an express loan, you're not using your personal collateral. You just put a down payment of 10 percent into your business checking account. The SBA then dumps the $150,000, or whatever you need, into that account.

When talking about the service industries, this is a perfect option—very simple, very easy to do. However, it's not an option if you're going to do a bricks-and-mortar franchise. That's more of a build-out. You're going to be looking at more of an SBA 7(a) loan, the transaction for which will be a little more in-depth. With that, you can borrow up to $5 million with from 20 percent to 30 percent down, depending on what you're doing. As you build up, the SBA pays out the money to you over time as you go through the building process and as you need it. With SBA loans like that, you'll likely need a credit score of 680 to 690, and it generally takes anywhere from two to four months to get it done.

Term loans, which a number of lenders provide, have very good interest rates, but approval is going to come down to your good credit. Our funding partners like franchises. Franchises have a good track record of success. Of course, if a franchise you're looking at does not have a good track record, then you probably shouldn't be looking at it anyway and you may not be able to get a loan for it.

You can also go the portfolio loan route. It takes from two to three weeks, and you can borrow up to about 80 percent of your account balance for portfolio loans. You're looking at providing a minimum security deposit of about $85,000. Your stocks should be trading at about $5 per share or more. No minimum credit score is required for a portfolio loan.

UNSECURED AND BLENDED LOANS

There are also unsecured loans, which are a little bit different. What is an unsecured loan? An unsecured loan is a credit card. Yes, you can actually get a loan through credit cards. Now, there are good and bad ways of using credit cards, and you have to be really careful with the credit card you get. My lenders will find you credit cards that give you zero percent APR, for a dollar limit or an amount of time. You have to make certain that if you're using those, you can pay them off in a certain amount of time so that you're not stuck with high credit card interest rates.

Another type of loan you can get is a working capital loan, although you have to execute the franchise agreement first before you can get one. Again, a 680 to 690 credit score, 10 percent down, and no collateral is what you need, but it is pretty fast funding, taking thirty days or so.

You can also do equipment leasing. With equipment leasing, you're generally looking at about $10,000. Equipment leasing takes a higher credit score, in the 700 range. Leasing companies also want you to have been in business for a couple of years, which is a little challenging. If you're in business for, like, zero to two years, you'll need the higher credit score, but if you've been in business a little while longer, the required credit score goes down to about 650.

PRETTY GOLDEN

I know all these things because I work with my funding people quite often. I'm not a complete expert in funding, which is why I have experts who help me. What we will do for you, if you're interested in looking into funding your franchise, is put you in front of my people, who will get you the information you need. We'll go over it with you. You don't have to go with the lender we introduce you to—there may be two or three others you want to look at. You may want to compare and see which one is best for what you are trying to do.

When I started looking at franchises, I was just thinking, *How am I going to afford this thing? I'm going to go bankrupt if I'm not careful and invest in a franchise without enough money.* Well, I found out my 401(k) was available. Then it was just a matter of, *Well, how much do I have in my 401(k)?* Then my franchise consultant went back and looked at the different franchises that were within the amount of money I had to invest. Once I found that 401(k)s were possible, that opened up a few different franchises that I could look at because now I had more to invest.

It's the same when I work with my folks. If you don't have the cash for it up front, that's one of the first questions we'll go over: how you are going to pay for it? Then we'll take you through a few more:

- Are you OK with getting a loan if you don't have a 401(k) plan?

- If you do have a 401(k) or other retire plans, are you OK with using your retirement money to get into the franchise?

- Now that we've covered the benefits of each option, the most important question is: what do you feel more comfortable with?

Overall, I felt more comfortable not going into debt.

I believed in myself. I followed that franchise—after all, I had investigated enough of them. I believed that I could actually get in, make it happen, and make it work for me. That's why I went with using my retirement money. I started out with a certain amount and ended up with ten times that amount after about nine years. But again, a 401(k) rollover is not for everybody.

Using other people's money, from my investor's point of view, seems to be a nice and lucrative thing to do. You never have to worry about investing your own as long as the business generates more income than your expenses, including that loan payment. Then you are pretty golden. My investors always look at whether a business can "service the debt."

A COMPLETE CHANGE

Let's take a look at Steve. He enjoyed working with others, so much so that his degree was in hospitality management. He was already managing a restaurant when we connected. He genuinely struck me as a great people person. As we had our calls together and as I got him through the process, I could tell that he enjoyed meeting and talking with others. He was very personable, and he really liked running his business. Throughout his career, he was on a path of self-improvement; likewise, he was passionate about bettering his employees' educations through training and hard work.

Years before, Steve had started his own pizza shop and grew it independently. While he was passionate about his shop and team, life threw some surprises into the picture. Everything was going well until he got a divorce. As he made his way along the ups and downs of senior management, something was becoming clear: he didn't have the time he wanted to spend with his kids. Added to that was the fact that even though he was working such long hours, he was not making the money he needed to build a better future for his family.

Once it all began to feel unstable, he wanted to do something different. Not having time to spend with his kids as they grew older meant he would miss out on all the experiences and activities he would like to one day treasure. This was not an option. So, he figured he could expand his role by pivoting into a franchise in the restaurant industry. That's when he came to me. As with Paula from Chapter 2, things went a little differently for Steve.

Steve was ready to change his life. At first, he thought that change might include the restaurant industry. As we spoke, I could tell he was looking for the next best thing. While I could understand that he wanted to stay where he was most familiar, I wanted to help him avoid the mistake of keeping his search only to what was in fashion.

When we started talking about the different industries that were available to him, I wanted him to see how he could use his skill set in those different industries. As it ultimately turned out, beyond skill sets and trends, most franchises were not right for him, as he did not like paying royalties. So, we found Steve a business opportunity in the medical field that didn't require a whole lot of money—only about $50,000.

It was a very easy business opportunity, requiring only an unsecured loan through credit cards. Steve decided to go that route. He didn't want to pay out a whole lot of extra money to get his business going, but this opportunity wouldn't require a whole lot. He needed about $45,000 a year or more. He was perfectly happy with that.

My funding partners found him a few different credit card companies. Steve went in and used those credit cards to purchase the business opportunity, and then turned around and paid them off right away. He was able to build his business quickly enough to pay off the unsecured debt before he incurred any interest. He didn't stop there! He's continuing to grow his medical franchise quite well, and he was able to secure real freedom in that he could spend more time with his kids, creating memories, and being the father he needed to be.

Over the course of Chapters 1 to 5, I've touched on a few different pieces of the process. Now that I've covered the details through the investment itself, I'd like to pull it all together with a quick look at our six-step process of investing. Of course, as it did for Patricia and her dad in Chapter 4, sometimes the journey includes an exciting round of bowling with future friends and colleagues. Keep reading to discover more!

CHAPTER 6

THE PROCESS OF INVESTING

In our last chapter, we talked about our funding process to finance your franchises. In previous chapters, we also talked about the different types of franchises that you could get into—single unit, area developer, and master franchises. We've gone through a few non-franchise opportunities as well: business opportunities. That should give you a general feel for the different types of franchises that you can get into and the different things that you can do. We also looked at a couple of people who have looked into franchises and their backgrounds. In this chapter, we're going to go through our actual process.

So, what is the process we undertake? You and I will go through it together to find franchises that will fit your goals and your criteria. What I want you to do is get a feel for exactly the kind of questions we're going to be asking, what we're looking for, why we're asking them, and how I am going to use that information to then find franchises that fit what you are trying to accomplish. The main goal here is to look at where you have been, where you are now, and where you want to be five or ten years from now. We're going to go through all that together. This is not just for me; this should hold for any good franchise consultant you get in contact with.

Rick came to me after he'd looked into franchises independently. Previously, he owned a couple of his own businesses, and before that he worked for a corporation. After being a marketing director for some time, he went into business for himself as a business development consultant. He enjoyed working with teams, interacting with clients, and creating proposals. Ultimately, similar to my situation, he found he wasn't exactly where he wanted to be. He needed something that was going to help him out.

Rick was looking for a flexible schedule. On top of that, he wanted the ability to interact with clients and plan solutions for their problems. He wanted influence over proposals, pricing, and executive planning. As you can imagine, he didn't like the corporate world, which is why he started a couple of his own businesses. More specifically, he felt that corporate decision-making limited success and flexibility.

He eventually reached the point where he realized he was unable to find a franchise that fit his needs. He did not have the time to go through all the available options to determine which was right for him. When he decided he needed help and guidance, he reached out to me. So, what did we do with Rick? As with everyone I work with, we started with an initial phone call.

STEP 1: THE INITIAL CALL

Again, this goes for any good franchise consultant you're working with. I'm going to ask you things like, "Is this a specific inquiry or a general inquiry?" Maybe you've got something specific in mind that you'd like answered or that you're looking at and you need some help investigating a specific franchise or business. Or maybe you don't know anything about franchising, so this is more of a general inquiry. On my side of things, I'm really looking to get answers to a few questions:

- What kind of experience have you had looking into franchising?

- What are you expecting to get out of a franchise?

- What do you see the franchise doing for you?

It's important to express those points pretty quickly because we need to know if your expectations are reasonable. Most of the time, my clients have fairly reasonable expectations. From time to time, they want to replace their incomes. For anyone with an annual income of $250,000 who wants to replace it within the first year, a startup franchise is probably not going to do that. But this begs the following questions.

- What do you see a franchise doing for you?
- What is it about a franchise that appeals to you?
- What has you looking into a franchise at this point in your life?

In terms of recurring expectations, some people want the franchise to supply them with all the clients. They do not want to have to find clients on their own. Frankly, this isn't really a reasonable expectation, although some franchises are better at generating business than others.

Ultimately, what we'll be going through is really getting to know each other. I want you to ask questions about me and about franchising. In the end, it's going to come down to you feeling good about having me help you with the franchise selection and investigation. "Do you like and trust me enough at this time to move forward with that?" That's what that first initial phone call is all about.

Another thing I'm going to look at is how much time and money you are looking to invest, because those are the two major points along the way: (1) time and (2) money. It doesn't matter if you have a little bit or a lot of time to invest—we've got franchises that are absentee, or semi-absentee, and ones that require a full-time commitment. We can find something for you in any industry with those expectations in mind.

The other thing is, of course, the financial requirements—each franchise has different requirements for liquidity and net worth. Basically, you're looking at coming up with a franchise fee, which is going to be around $50,000 in cash. Most franchisors are looking for individuals with a net worth of $200,000 or more. To get around that, you need to be willing to get a loan. We can see what you qualify for and find franchises that fit within those qualifications.

Getting into the service industry probably requires the least amount of investment. You are looking at needing about $50,000 in cash and having a net worth of $200,000 or more. I'll ask you, "Is that you? Are you good with that and, if not, are you OK with getting a loan?" Then you're going to share your goals, expectations, and what you're trying to accomplish with me.

I will answer any questions that you have about me and my background—my franchising background and business background—and anything else you need or want to know so that you can get to know me better. If by this point you haven't hung up on me and said, "No way am I working with this dude," and I find your expectations to be reasonable, you'll then move forward with me to step 2.

We need to get to know each other and set our expectations. After that first call, if I haven't done so already, I'll send you background information on me and the team I work with, so you can look us over and make sure you're comfortable working with us. I'll also send you an email titled "Your Preparation for Our Upcoming Call on Franchising Options." This covers the due diligence process that I will take you through so we can find franchises that are a good fit for you. We'll investigate those franchises, so you get the information you need to make an informed decision. We also have a matrix of business types, which we will go over as well (see Chapter 2).

As part of your preparation for the upcoming call on franchising, we provide a link to a questionnaire. Filling that out will be your next step after our initial call. I'm gathering as much information as I can about you, to get to know you as well as I can. So, give me some background information on yourself. Tell me a little bit about yourself. Brag about yourself. You've made it this far in life. You've done something good.

There are also questions about your finances. As I indicated before, each franchise sets certain qualifications for their candidates because, in essence, they do not want you to run out of money. They know from previous experience that you have to have at least *this much* cash and at least *that much* net worth, so you won't run out of money. If you don't want to list your cash and net worth on the form, that's all right—you can tell me about them later. I ask those questions so I can find franchises that not only fit your background and personality but also where you are financially. This way, I don't come back to you with ones where you're like, "There's no way I can afford that...."

STEP 2: DUE DILIGENCE—ALL ABOUT YOU

The next step is all about you. Our second call will last for about thirty minutes to an hour, and it is going to be all about you. We're going to go over the questionnaire that you already filled out and sent to me, and the matrix of business types. We're really looking at where you have been, where you are now, and where you want to be. That way, I know what you bring to the table (and so do you) and what's going on in your life now that you've decided a franchise is the way to go. Then we'll discuss what you see a franchise doing for you.

We're going to go through how you will pay for the investment. As I indicated in the previous chapter, a lot of people like to use other people's money to get a franchise and to build it up. That, of course, is up to you. At that point, if you'd like to look at loans, I'll introduce you to our funding folks, who do franchise funding all the time. Franchises are pretty darn easy to fund. I've never had any issues funding a franchise before. It's all just going to come down to your credit score.

The next question is whether you're going to have anybody else involved in this process. Do you have a spouse who wants to be involved? In our phone calls, we can always put the spouse on the phone with us. Usually, a good idea is to have everybody who's going to be involved in the decision-making process on that phone call when we talk.

STEP 3: MAKE A MATCH

Once I have done that and I've gathered as much information as I can about you, the next step is making a match. Now that you and I have talked, that's it for you. You get to sit back and wait for a couple of days—it's time for me to do all the work. Three, four, or five matches is what I'm looking for in franchises that fit what you are looking to accomplish. I work with about three hundred different franchises and communicate by phone with them all the time. We already know who they are looking for in a potential franchisee.

Now I've just got to take your information and see which of those you're looking for that are also looking for you, and that's when I make the matches. That is where my big challenge comes in. I will come up with a few different matches for you, and we will sit down and review the opportunities together. That will happen on our next phone call. We will talk about each one, what your role is going to be, the background of the franchise, and why I feel it's a good fit for you. We're also going to determine which franchises you would like to investigate further. We'd like to take those four or five franchises and reduce them down to two, and then we put you on the phone with those franchises.

STEPS 4 & 5: REVIEW AND NARROW DOWN OPPORTUNITIES

I had Alison come to me at one point. She was in the corporate world, working as a business manager, and wasn't too happy with her corporate situation. Alison had a background as a controller, and she had a degree in accounting. We went through the process together, and I came up with four or five ideas for her. She liked the ideas, and she was interested in all of them but especially in the martial arts studio I showed her. She said, "I really like working with kids. I really like seeing kids active and being proactive in kids' lives.

Alison was really surprised I came up with that idea, and she said, "I never would've thought about that had you not shown it to me." That's what I do. I try to get down into your depths to figure out what makes you feel good in life. As you look at franchises, I try to show you something that maybe you never would've thought about before. If you go out and try to look for franchises on your own, there are some things you may not think about. I may also pick out options for you that would make you say, "That does not resonate with me." I'm not perfect, but I try very hard. I wanted my idea to resonate with Alison, and she was quite surprised.

We can go back and forth a few times to give you some time to look over your franchise opportunities. We do things on your time schedule. So, once we do get to the point when you have picked out a couple of franchises that you could go with, we'll also take a look at funding the franchise and how you're going to pay for it. I will also introduce you to our funding people. The franchise investigation process generally takes from six to eight weeks, depending on how fast or slow you want to go. Funding may take about the same time.

STEP 6: FRANCHISE INVESTIGATION PROCESS

Now, legally, you must have the franchise disclosure documents (more on FDDs in Chapter 7) in your hands for two weeks before you can purchase a franchise. Franchisors are going to take you through a process just like I did—they get to know you and you get to know them. They're going to take you through their operations and training manuals and explain how they're going to do the marketing, how they're going to get you clients, and how they find employees. They will also show you how to find employees yourself.

They'll go through everything that's involved in their franchise, so you get a good feel for that business. You're going to learn some of the background of the franchise, who's running it, their backgrounds, any legal issues, any bankruptcies, and—if they collect the financial data on their franchises—their financial performance. They will provide you a list of all the people who are currently running the franchise, as well as the people who started the franchise and are no longer running it.

We like to see an 85 to 90 percent success rate or better with franchises. There are many different reasons people are not successful at franchises, and you can find out what happened with the people who failed by asking the franchise. What happened with them? Why did they fail? But most importantly, you'll be able to call upon all of the franchisees in that system. You can call every single one you want. This can be a daunting process, especially if they're one of the bigger franchises and they've got one hundred, two hundred, or a thousand franchisees.

What you want once you start talking with the franchisees is to hear the same thing over and over again. You will realize, *OK, maybe I don't need to talk to too many more*, but you'll want to get a good feel for the franchise, so you get almost the same answers to your questions, with slight variations. The franchise will go over with you how they will help get you started and how they will support you. You'll want to verify all that information with the franchisees when you're talking with them.

If you are thinking you want to be the most successful franchisee in the system that they've ever had, then it would be a good idea for you to talk with their most successful franchisees and see if you can relate to them. Find out what they do. What is a day in the life of a franchisee like? Can you relate to that in general? Can you picture yourself doing that?

If so, then you're probably on the right track. If not, then go hire somebody else to do that work for you or move on to another franchise system. But again, in those franchise disclosure documents, you're going to have that ability to call upon those franchisees, and keep in mind when you're talking to the franchisees that you're making friends. Those are the people who are going to help you become successful. The more successful each one of those franchisees is, the more successful other franchisees become. The name becomes known, and the entire system is better for it as well. You're getting that name out there, and you're not competing with each other because you're working different territories, so you're all helping each other grow.

You have now had a chance to talk to many franchisees and look over the franchise disclosure documents. This has taken six to eight weeks, depending on how fast or slow you wanted to go. Some people take longer than others—it just depends on you. After all of your due diligence, it is now time to go meet the franchisors in person.

You're going to go to what they call their "meet the team day" or "discovery day," which is when you visit the offices of the franchise. You meet those people face to face who are going to help you become successful and you ask all the difficult questions, get to know them, and do a good gut check. Make sure they are the type of people you want to be working with over the next five to ten years. Make sure you see yourself being successful with them, because they're the folks who are really going to help you out.

Now keep in mind that at this point the only thing you have to sign is the franchise disclosure document to confirm that you received it. The franchise must have a receipt saying, "Yes, I received the FDD on this date." No money is to change hands. You're just gathering information.

Discovery day is when you gather the final bit of information. You're not necessarily going to be signing up on discovery day. You can, but that is not usual. You need to have a franchise attorney look over the paperwork before you sign the franchise agreements. Discovery day is a time to get to know everybody in person who is going to be helping you grow your business.

DISCOVERY DAY

Discovery day is an event that usually lasts a day or two, and you can really get to know the franchisors on a personal level. They'll take you out to dinner or lunch. Some take you out to all sorts of different things so you can really get to know each other, which allows you to again make certain that they are the type of people you want to be working with at the end of the day. For Patricia's dad, in Chapter 4, the team took him bowling. He had a great time, and they went with the franchise that took him out bowling.

After discovery day, it's decision time. I will have sent you a franchise attorney to review all of your documents. It's always a good idea to have attorneys review your documents before you sign anything.

RIGHT AT HOME

Overall, Rick was looking for something he could do alongside the businesses he was currently running, something absentee or semi-absentee. He didn't actually want to work *in* the business itself. He was more for working *on* the business so that he could grow his team of people. What we looked at were his expectations. While he only had partial funds for what he wanted to accomplish, that wouldn't stop him.

Rick wanted to add to his portfolio of businesses. He didn't like the corporate world, and he specifically wanted to grow a business that would allow him to spend more time with his kids. He didn't want to do the corporate thing. Overall, by coming to us, Rick was already avoiding the big mistake of not making use of free experts, but he had already paid the price of doing it all on his own. Also, had he continued alone, he may have come to assume his financial situation meant he couldn't proceed into the franchising world at all.

Rick already had a good idea that franchising could be right for him. He just needed help finding the right one, and he needed to find the money to invest in it. He took the first step of coming to me. I was able to put him in touch with the local SCORE chapter. With a couple of businesses already on the side, he knew he wanted a big territory. We found Rick a service industry franchise that matched well with a couple of the businesses he was already doing. He also wanted to go out and meet with clients but not necessarily have to work *in* the business, as the business itself would do the work for him. He wanted to work more *on* it, potentially having a manager do some of the work for him, such as contacting clients.

We found him in a nice service industry with three territories. Rick has picked up his first one already. He picked out an area-developer plan, but he didn't quite have the money for it all at once. We got him the funding he needed for multiple territories of a home services franchise that was a great fit for him. At the time of writing, he was working on his SBA loan, and he was ready to shortly pick up two more territories.

We've gone through the steps of what a franchise consultant is going to do for you:

- Find new things that maybe you never thought of before
- Get to know you and what you're looking for
- Get to where you've been, where you are, and where you want to be
- Make the right match
- Come up with ideas for you that will fit what you are trying to accomplish
- Make certain, as we go through this process, that you're getting the information you need to make an informed decision

All those processes the franchisor explained to you, you're going to do with your franchise. You and I will be getting together again once a week, and we will go over all the information you collected from the franchises throughout the whole six- to eight-week period. However often you have questions, we will get together.

I'll check up on you, see how you're doing, and see if you're getting your questions answered. I will be with you through that entire process. At any point in time, if you don't want to talk to a franchise anymore and decide it wasn't for you, you can tell them, or you can tell me and I can tell them. I take care of all that.

You need funding people? I get funding people for you. You need a franchise attorney? I get franchise attorneys over to you. I will be with you through that entire process as we go through the investigation, talking about what you've learned, what you like, and what you don't like. We really want you to be successful.

If you're successful, you'll be more likely to tell your friends about me and about how I helped you through the process. I'm always happy to meet with more people! That's how I get most of my business—referrals from folks like you who have been successful in their franchise systems. So, of course we want to make certain that you make the right decision and that you are successful in your franchise.

Rick is very happy with what he's doing now with his franchise, and he is having fun with his two kids—and has a new one on the way. We're going to be bringing him a couple of more territories pretty soon. The last time I spoke with Rick, he was a bit too busy to talk for very long. "Business is great," he said. He's constantly getting new contracts, building a great business on his terms, and giving his family the life he wanted for them.

In Step 6, I mentioned FDDs a few times. You might be wondering what goes into those, which is great. We'll get further into what you should look for in those documents in the next chapter.

CHAPTER 7

WHAT TO LOOK FOR

In the last chapter, we went through how to find the perfect franchise for you: the initial call, the due diligence, making a match, reviewing opportunities, narrowing down options, investigating franchises (franchise disclosure documents), discovery day, and decision time. Now it is time to go more in-depth into what to look for with franchise disclosure documents. What should you be looking for in an FDD?

> For a deeper look, go over to my website, franchisemaven.com, and you can further review the FDD guidelines.

Before meeting me, Sam had been a regional business manager for a large firm, and he managed a large sales team. Unfortunately, his position was eliminated. Up to that point, he had really enjoyed his work. Outside his career he enjoyed coaching children's soccer, fishing, and the great outdoors. I could tell he was a great guy who loved life.

Now that he was thinking about the future, he knew he didn't want to work for someone else. He wanted to create his own team. He wanted something that was enjoyable, with plenty of schedule flexibility.

Sam wanted to replace his income right away, and he needed a six-figure income to start off with. In order for Sam to get a realistic view of his income potential, I had him speak with many different franchisees. Once Sam started speaking with them, he really opened up to the idea of franchising.

We found Sam the perfect franchise. As he communicated with people who were already involved, he was able to see how much each franchisee and each of the top owners were making. He pictured himself doing what the top owners were doing and said, "Yep, I can do that. That's me. I can picture myself doing that. I feel it." With a realistic view of how soon the money would be coming in and how much it would be, he was then able to plan his investment.

We started putting him into the franchise and went through negotiating his contract. We got him a franchise attorney, and the franchise attorney said, "Ah." Sam wanted two territories. He wanted bigger shots. He knew he could take on more than that. He felt that good about the business. Well, the franchise agreement included a franchise fee and a territory fee for each territory.

When my franchise attorney looked at that, he said, "That is not normal. That is actually highly unusual. The territory fee is fine. You get a territory fee for each territory. That part works. The franchise fee—just because you're buying two territories, why are you paying two franchise fees? You're only buying one franchise. You're buying two territories, one franchise. So why is there a territory fee and a franchise fee for both territories?"

That didn't make any sense, and this is exactly why it's important to work with the right people. It was time to look further into the situation. It's hard to know what you don't know. To help you gain at least an idea of what's involved with an FDD, let's now take a look at some of the details together.

FDD ITEMS 1–4

In an FDD, there are twenty-three items. You're going to be looking at items 1 through 4 for background information on the franchise system itself, on the people who run the franchise. When we get to that point, you need to be comfortable with their backgrounds, making certain that they know what they're doing when it comes to either franchising or the industry, or both.

Also, within items 1 through 4, you'll find their litigation and potential bankruptcy history. We don't want to see any litigation or bankruptcies at all. It's not a good sign when we see them, although generally speaking, with litigation the more franchises you get, the more chances someone has faced litigation. So, if they've got 500 to 1,000 franchises, it is very likely somebody attempted to sue them for something. This is just the nature of the beast. Look at that and get information on what happened and how it was resolved. Make sure there are no major problems going on.

Item 2 red flags: Check the backgrounds of the people running the franchise. How much experience do they have in the industry? Are there any past issues, such as being involved in failed businesses?

Item 3 red flags: Be alert for multiple lawsuits filed by franchisees alleging fraud or misrepresentation on the part of the franchisor. Is there a pending class action suit by franchisees or consumers that, if successful, could bankrupt the company?

Item 4 red flag: Has anyone been bankrupt in the past?

FDD ITEMS 5–9

Items 5 and 6 are the fees charged by the franchisor. They are fairly self-explanatory. Item 7 is important because that is going to be the estimate of the investment required to establish the business. The total investment is going to vary depending on the type of franchise and location—so the FDD will break down the total investment of what you pay, to whom you pay it, and when. Make sure you are well capitalized. Do not assume this is everything needed to get the business started. Talk with other franchisees and find out if they spent above and beyond this amount to get started. Get your accountant involved as well.

Item 8 is going to give you restrictions on the purchase of the products to be used and sold in the unit. Again, that just depends on if you're selling things and, if so, where you get the products from, and so on. Item 9 is the franchisee's obligations, your obligations to the franchise itself. Look for any large rebates the franchise receives. Are they making more off the rebates than they are from royalties? Make sure the price of what you have to buy is fair.

Also make sure the FDD and the franchise agreement are the same.

FDD ITEMS 10 & 11

Item 10 stipulates if franchisor financing is available. Every once in a while, we see franchisors do financing, but not very often. If they do, it will be pretty much the same as borrowing from a bank, requiring credit checks. If you default, the franchise can terminate your franchise agreement. Item 11 is the summary of the services the franchise provides relative to the franchise, including training, site selection, marketing, and providing technology systems. Site selection is important if you're doing something like a bricks-and-mortar type of franchise. You are not an expert on site selection, on real estate, or lease negotiation. You will want them to do those things for you, so make certain that they do. This also involves marketing expenses. Are they charging for this? If so, how much involvement do you have?

FDD ITEM 12

Item 12 covers territorial protections. Most franchises give you territorial protection. What that means is that no other franchisees of this franchise will be allowed to market or do business with any clients within your protected territory. That protected territory is going to vary depending on whether or not you have a bricks-and-mortar franchise, which generally entails a per-mile radius around it—as opposed to a service industry franchise, for which they generally give you a population set that they're looking for. Make sure the territories are outlined in the agreement.

FDD ITEMS 13–19

Items 13 and 14 cover the status of the franchise, trademarks, copyrights, and patents. Item 15 covers the obligations of the franchisee as they relate to participation in the business operation. If the franchise allows you to be passive or semi-passive, look for restrictions placed on your managers. Some require managers to own a share of your business. Item 16 covers restrictions on what can be sold by the franchisee. Again, this is going to vary. If you're running a retail-type franchise, there will be certain restrictions on what can be sold and what cannot be sold. Make sure all trademarks are registered.

Item 17 covers renewal, termination, transfer, and dispute resolution. Renewals are probably one of the more important things that people look at in item 17. What does it take to renew the franchise? Maybe $2,500? Maybe $5,000? Generally, not a whole lot, but make sure you're aware of the cost. Item number 18 covers any public figures who are used in a local franchise, if applicable.

Item 19 provides a description of the financial information. This is when people ask me, "What can I make with the franchise?" Legally, I cannot tell you that. The Federal Trade Commission regulates that quite heavily, so only franchises can tell you that and only if they have it in item number 19.

If they don't mention any financial performances in item 19, they cannot by law discuss financial performance with you. We can still get that information, but we'll just get it from the franchisees instead of from the franchise.

Make sure the financial information is from the franchisees, which will give you a better view, as opposed to just getting it from corporate locations.

FDD ITEM 20

Item 20 shows you the current and former franchisees. What this one goes into is how many people are currently running the business. Also, how many people started the business and are no longer running the business?

Now, there can be many reasons for people starting a business but no longer running it. Maybe they had to move. One family member got the franchise, but another one was still working in corporate. The corporate job moved, so everybody had to move. That could happen. Or illness, or many other different things. Find out why these people left. What's the story behind them?

Franchisees on your list to call will be those who are currently running the business. It might be time-consuming to call everyone if there are a thousand franchisees. But, as I mentioned in a former chapter, what we're looking for when we call the franchisees is consistent feedback. You should be hearing the same thing over and over again. Once you get to that point, you'll know you've gained a good idea of what's going on.

Also, it is simple math to calculate their success rate. I would like to see an 85–90 percent success rate or better on these franchises. Check that out. And as I mentioned before, when you're calling these franchisees after you get the FDD, you are going to make a lot of friends along the way. It's a good way to make friends.

FDD ITEMS 21–23

Item 21 provides their financial statements. Item number 22 covers their contracts and item 23 their receipts.

It is best to have your CPA look over the financial statements. Look for where the franchise makes most of its money. It should be through royalties. The better you do, the better it does. However, a red flag should go up if most of the money comes from franchise sales or product rebates. Good franchises sustain themselves on royalties.

IMPORTANT DETAILS

By law, you must have the FDDs in your hands for two weeks before you can invest in a franchise. So, for the most part this would be the only thing they have you sign before you go into the actual franchise agreements themselves. What you sign is just a receipt saying, "Yes, I received it on this date." You have no obligation to actually purchase that franchise. It's just showing that you received the FDDs. They can then show that, by law, you've had the FDDs in your hands for at least two weeks before you purchase the franchise itself. Some companies do it manually by mail—most do it electronically.

So, what are you looking for in the FDDs? You're looking for what industry they're in, and what kinds of experiences the franchises have in this industry. What's their background? What makes them stand out? Can you say, "Yeah, these folks here, they know what they're doing, and I believe in them"? Because that's a big thing—you've got to believe in these folks.

Now, when going through the FDDs, always have an attorney look over them. I always send two or three different attorneys for you to choose between. I have some people I recommend, but it's up to you whether you use the ones I recommend or whether you use somebody else.

After that, you're going to be able to talk to all of the franchisees who are currently running their franchise businesses. You will want to learn the processes for the franchisors and the franchise itself—all of their processes, up to and including how they are going to get you clients. How are they going to help you operate your business, increase your profits, and increase your bottom line? If you're in the service industry, you'll want to look at how they will get you workers. If you're going into something where you are doing home services, such as tuning up kitchens or redoing garages, you're not necessarily the one who will do the work yourself. You should be going out and getting clients. What you need is a franchise system that's going to help you get workers.

You should see if how you go about getting those workers is outlined in their processes, in their steps, or in their FDDs. Do they have a process by which they say you need contractors or employees for what you're going to do? Because if you want to work with the clients, you will want to turn the work over to somebody else. Now, in a bricks-and-mortar franchise it's pretty simple—you just put out a "For Hire" sign.

If you're working for something medical, then yes, you may need some help from the franchisor to find workers. Some of our handyman franchises have a great system: they provide you with a questionnaire and tell you where you need to share it online. You're going to get applicants by following their process. You'll then narrow it down to the four or five people you want to interview.

That not only goes for your home services—that also goes for your senior care when you're hiring the caregivers. But if you have to hire employees, especially in the service industries, you need the franchisor to help you find the right people. Look for it in the FDDs. Look for it in their systems and processes. They should have a system for you to go out and find the employees you will need to work for you, either as contractors or as employees.

If you're going to run your franchise in a semi-passive way, find out if there are any restrictions in the FDDs. Can you hire a manager? Do they have a management team that they can send to you? How do they help you find a manager? Is there a system or process in place? Or, if you are going to run it in a semi-absentee way, where do you go and look for staff? How do you look for the best people? That's something to look for when you're going through the investigation process with the franchise. Where have they outlined that in the FDDs? Always read it.

We pointed out how territories, franchise fees, royalties, and ad funds are covered in the FDDs. They're also going to be in the franchise agreement. Once we get to the franchise agreement, you definitely need a franchise attorney with experience looking at FDDs.

NEGOTIATIONS (NICE AND SIMPLE)

We found the perfect franchise for Sam. He didn't want a nine-to-five, everyday job. He wanted to find something that was enjoyable. That was his big thing. So, we found something in the services industry for him. These are some of the things we went through with Sam: the FDDs and franchise agreement, how to go about finding employees, and how the franchise would help him make things a lot simpler. That's why you pay the franchise fee and the royalties—you're looking for a nice, easy, and simple process.

With a territory, some things are negotiable, and some things are nonnegotiable in the franchise agreement, and that's where a good franchise attorney comes in. Keep in mind I am not an attorney, and I cannot give you any legal advice whatsoever. That is why you need a good franchise attorney to look through the whole agreement and look for things that stand out. This is not like a job when you go into a corporation where everybody's paid differently. When you go into a corporation, you can negotiate. However badly they need somebody at that point in time, you have leverage to negotiate your salary.

When I worked in corporate, they did not really appreciate it if you discussed salaries with other employees. They discouraged that sort of thing. A franchise agreement is just the opposite—they want everybody on the same level playing field. There won't be much in the franchise agreement itself that is negotiable. Keep in mind that if everybody negotiated their own terms on franchise agreements, once you got up to 100 or 500 franchisees it would be a nightmare to keep track of all of them. Instead, they keep everybody on exactly the same level.

While there's not much that can be negotiated in a franchise agreement, there are some. Territory is one of them. You could add a few more ZIP codes if you like, but again, consult a franchise attorney if you do. I have not ever seen a franchise fee negotiated, but lately some franchises have been changing their franchise fees in return for a different royalty structure. So that's a possibility.

But generally speaking, franchise fees and royalties are not negotiable. Occasionally, during hard times, I did see a couple of franchises that did not require the payment of royalties for three to six months. It comes down to the old saying, "It doesn't hurt to ask. The worst they can do is say no." However, I don't often see royalties negotiated, as that's how a franchise stays in business. And you want them to stay in business because you want them to stay on top of what's happening in the franchise world and in their industry and to keep you abreast of it.

The ad fund is another thing—some franchises have one, some franchises don't. Make sure you're aware of it. It'll be in both the franchise agreement and the FDDs. It may or may not be negotiable. I've seen that sometimes franchises will waive it for a while, but generally not.

DISCLAIMER:

I'm not an attorney—get an attorney's advice. My advice concerns the franchises I work with, and I work with about 300 different ones, but there are at least 4,000 out there. I cannot speak for every single franchise. I can just speak from my experience in the franchise world over the last nine years.

WHAT'S NEGOTIABLE AND WHAT'S NOT?

The first right of refusal applies when you buy a territory. Maybe you're thinking about getting more than one territory, but you really want to try one out first—to see how it works for you. Make sure you're comfortable with it and can get it going before you take on too big of a job. That's a perfect idea. The first right of refusal says that if somebody is looking at the territory adjacent to yours, the franchisor must tell you about it and give you a set amount of time, maybe a week or two, to come up with the money for that territory before somebody else can buy it.

Negotiating a reduction of your royalty or a reduction of your ad fund is possible sometimes. It just depends on the franchise. A good franchise attorney will help you understand what is negotiable and what is not and will work with you to get good things negotiated. Most importantly, what a franchise attorney does is look through the FDDs and franchise agreements for things that are out of place.

THE NECESSITY OF A GOOD FRANCHISE ATTORNEY

Sam's situation demonstrates exactly why you get a good franchise attorney who can spot these things. As a reminder, our attorney discovered an abnormal franchise fee charged per territory. He went back to the franchisors and said, "This is highly unusual. This doesn't look right. Let's waive that franchise fee for that other territory since he's only buying one franchise. So, one franchise fee, two territory fees."

Our attorney got it waived. The franchise subsequently changed its franchise agreements and FDDs. We got Sam out of that extra franchise fee, which made him even happier since he saved quite a bit more money than he thought he would. Who could possibly complain about paying less than you thought you needed to?

Sam got his two territories, and he is in the home services industry and is living happily ever after. I think we ended up saving him about $15,000 on that second territory. In terms of freedom, not only was he able to replace his income but he also now has the joy of not worrying about having his position eliminated again. And it wasn't enough! Today, he's looking to open more franchises in the home services industry that complement his new workload and life.

You can review the FDD guidelines on my website. Again, I'm not giving legal advice—franchise attorneys help with that sort of thing. I will recommend some to you, and you can find others on your own. And, of course, there is life beyond the FDDs! In the next chapter, let's take a look at the next steps after investing.

CHAPTER 8

NEXT STEPS AFTER INVESTING

So, you just invested in a franchise, you've gone through the entire process with me, and we found a franchise for you. You're loving it, you signed the agreements, and you paid the franchise fee. What's next?

Brian was a sales manager when he found me. He liked his team and his clients, and he was putting his marketing degree to good use. In life, he loved fitness, being outside, spending time with his kids, and working around the house. While his personal life was beautiful, at work he was starting to feel some boredom. He realized that he needed something more challenging. He was going nuts doing the same thing over and over again, with no satisfaction.

Work takes up the majority of our lives. Brian was an active man who needed new challenges to keep him going. His first look into franchising was through connecting with me. That's a great start! As we communicated, it was clear that he had already dismissed some industries in which he assumed he couldn't possibly use his skill set. Something that caught my attention was the joy I saw when he mentioned how much he enjoyed working around his own house. With that insight, I took him in a new direction.

Once we started looking at home improvement franchises, he really started perking up. He did not know anything about the industry, so we went over it in detail. After he spoke with a couple of franchises, and then the franchisees, he knew it was the path he wanted to take.

We lined him up with a home equity line of credit. He invested in the franchises and started getting contracts as soon as his training was completed (which is Step 1). This brings me to what happens after investing:

1. Training
2. Coaching
3. Grand opening
4. Franchise meetings

STEP 1: TRAINING

The first thing you're going to do is some training at the franchise home office. I spent about three days on my training. Brian spent four. This will depend on the franchise itself. Different franchises are going to do different things. Mine was a telephone communications franchise; Brian's was more of a remodeling type of franchise.

So, mine was mostly all about paperwork, and they showed me exactly how their systems and processes work, in detail, throughout the day. Brian's training was about doing remodeling, so they went through the following with him:

- How to set up a project
- How to use their software systems
- How to enter data into their software systems
- How to present information to clients
- How to present the end product

- How to follow up with clients and bill them
- How to do collections
- And so on

As an example, the franchise actually flooded a room, gave him the equipment, and showed him exactly how to dry everything out with the fans going and how to take down the walls that were water-damaged.

You might not be the one who goes in and does the actual work, but you will learn how it is done and how to get it done. Some things you can do remotely, but for the most part you will go to their offices and learn everything there is to know: how to run the business, bookkeeping, payroll, calling on clients and what to say to them, how to market, and how to advertise. They're going to go through that entire process with you. I know that with some of the franchises you will start making phone calls right away to call potential clients. They'll show you exactly how to do it, what to say, what their process is, and how to book client appointments. They want you to right then be able to step into the business and go.

STEP 2: COACHING

When you've gone through the training, they're going to assign you a coach. They did with me, and they did with Brian as well. That coach will set up regular appointments with you—once a week, or once a day, whatever it takes. They will make sure that you're on track to start building the franchise. They will have given you goals and step-by-step processes as part of your training. They will go through them with you again, and they will make certain you are accomplishing the goals and following the processes on a regular basis.

You're not going to be getting up in the morning wondering, *What do I do next?* You will have a plan that's already in place. That is why you spend the money on a franchise and pay ongoing royalties. This is what you're getting—a partner who takes you through the process and will stay with you every step of the way.

Now, that mentor may be with you for a week or a few months. This will depend on you and how quickly you take on your new role. Your mentor will always be there to help you out, and you'll always have the franchise to call on—although different franchises handle that differently. They may make weekly calls to go over your goals, but that could happen as often as every day.

STEP 3: GRAND OPENING

Restaurant franchises, or any bricks-and-mortar franchises, will set up a grand opening for you, and a lot of the franchises will send reps to be there for the event. They'll do all the press releases, they'll do the marketing, they'll show you how to do it and who to talk to, and they'll get everything going for you in advance.

Fitness franchises will start helping you get clients right away, so that by the time your doors open you will already have fifty to one hundred clients who are ready to start using your fitness franchise that day or that week. The franchisors want you to get enough clients immediately so that your break-even point comes quickly.

STEP 4: FRANCHISE MEETINGS

Remember all those franchisees you called when you were trying to determine if a franchise system was a good fit for you? All those franchisees are now your friends. So, in addition to the franchisor helping you, you now have all the other franchisees in the business to call upon. They will give you advice on everything because if you grow, they grow, and if they grow, you grow. The whole system grows as more and more people know who you are. So, expect an extensive amount of training and an extensive amount of mentoring. That's what you should be looking for.

All franchises have meetings at least once a year where all the franchisees get together. The franchise is going to talk about the industry and any changes to it—anything new, anything different. They'll let you know how they will help you grow in the future. Always attend those meetings. They are a good way to get a lot of information.

When you're with all the other franchisees in the same room, talk to them about their businesses, how they're doing, what they're doing differently, and how they grow. You are not competing with each other, as you all have individual territories that no other franchisees can enter. You'll learn a lot of new things, make a lot of new friends, and work together toward realizing your mutual goals.

WHAT'S NEXT?
(EXIT STRATEGY OR CASH COW?)

This brings us to when you've now been in the business for a number of years. Now what? Do we need to craft an exit strategy? Are you thinking about building the business up to a certain point and then walking away from it, or do you want to make it a cash cow?

Maybe, to begin with, you need to establish an exit strategy. What are your plans for five to ten years down the road? That's one of the things we examine when we go over what you're looking to accomplish. Brian accomplished his goal. He made his dream of running his own business come true. He was getting tired of the corporate world and wanted to do something different, so we got him a franchise, and we got him trained. He got his first appointment right away and started growing from there.

He grew it up to where he said, three years later, "I really like my job after all, and I know how to run a business, so why don't I do both?" So, he ended up selling his remodeling business. He got a good chunk of money for it and got his job back (or another job similar to what he had before). Now we are looking at getting Brian another franchise that he can do semi-passively on the side, in addition to his other job. I did the same thing when I was an engineer, but eventually I realized I didn't want to do the job thing at all anymore. However, Brian decided to go back and do it. It's a personal choice.

We talked about Kat in Chapter 3. Kat was building up a large number of franchise units. He first had thirty-three, then sixty-one—he's putting together groups of franchises. Whenever he can buy a large territory—say six to ten locations—he puts a manager in place over it. He wants up to one hundred locations—that's ten managers. Each one of those managers will manage about fifty people, but Kat's only managing ten people because he only manages the managers. His is not an exit strategy; he wants to keep the business as a cash cow, rather than sell and get out.

Back to Brian: what he did was look at what it takes to sell a franchise. Selling a franchise is actually very simple. You just have to let the franchise know that you want to exit. You signed a ten-year agreement with the franchise, but that doesn't necessarily mean you have to stay in that franchise for ten years; you just turn over your franchise location, your territory, to somebody else.

You can get a business broker to do it. You can get me to do it. But once you let the franchise know, the franchise can let us franchise consultants know about it, and then we go out and find people for you. Most people sell a franchise for about three times the earnings before interest, taxes, and amortization (EBITA). A lot of times negotiations may start off a little bit higher, but all the franchise resells I've done—and I've done quite a few— typically sell for two-and-a-half to three times net. Check with your franchisor first, since obviously if any fees are involved, it's going to be in the franchise agreement. Generally, there will not be a whole lot of fees, but you'll find the information in the franchise agreement.

People do like to buy existing businesses, especially when the businesses are doing well. Once you've got your business doing quite well, it's very easy to find buyers for it. If you have any questions about that, stay tuned or reach out to me at franchisemaven.com.

Before I finish this book, I want to share a few more insights with you. Not many people think of this idea, but did you know that franchising is not limited to within national borders? International franchising is possible! In the final chapter, I will share more on this, along with other details you need to know.

CHAPTER 9

INTERNATIONAL FRANCHISING

Until this point, we've been talking about franchising as if it exists only in the U.S. I have news for you: it doesn't. Franchising takes place all over the world, and that means if you are not living in the U.S. and you want to come to the U.S., you can enter with an investor visa—an E-2 or EB-5 visa. We'll go over them—the details of what's required, the qualifications, and the investment levels on both.

If you don't want to come into the U.S., you can open up a franchise in another country and we'll go over that as well. Norma found me on LinkedIn. She had visited San Diego a couple of years earlier, and she absolutely fell in love with it. She was a finance director in Germany but really loved that sunny West Coast city. For two years she had no idea how she was going to get here, but obviously she needed a visa.

She saw on LinkedIn that I was a consultant and decided right then and there to reach out to me. We had a few nice conversations and she asked, "Greg, do you have an idea how to get me to California?" I answered, "Yes, indeed. I certainly do." And this is how we did it.

THE E-2 VISA

When you're looking at an E-2 visa, that is an investor visa. It allows foreign entrepreneurs to live and work in the U.S. through investments in a U.S. business. Spouses and unmarried children under the age of 21 may accompany investors to the U.S.

As I shared in the previous text box, these things do change on a regular basis, or at least every once in a while. We have visa attorneys who can walk you through this entire process and do everything for you. Some of the processes may be a little bit different, but for the most part, here are the general guidelines for coming into the U.S. Contact me and I will get you in front of a visa attorney who will give you the exact details of what's required. This is how it worked at the time of writing.

Investor visas are for treaty nationals only. There are probably more than eighty different countries that have treaties with the U.S. If you contact me, I'll email you a link to where you can find the list. You can also go to my website franchisemaven.com and look under E-2 visa and EB-5 green card. You will find a list of the countries that the U.S. has treaties with that allow people to come here.

You're usually granted visas in two- to five-year increments, depending on the treaty. How long can you stay here before a visa has to be renewed? Visas are renewable indefinitely, as long as the business continues. Every two to five years you renew it and as long as the business is continuing you can keep renewing. Again, you must have a passport from a treaty country, so go to my website or contact me and I'll give you the list or let you know if your country is on it.

What's the minimum investment? First off, you need to make a substantial investment in a qualifying business in the U.S. In practice, if you're looking at an E-2 visa, you need about $100,000 to have a strong E-2 visa case. A small investment may be possible depending on the nature of the business, but from what my attorneys tell me, about $100,000 makes a strong E-2 case.

Qualifying businesses include new or existing businesses. They can absolutely be new franchises. That's what Norma is doing in San Diego. You must have a minimum of 50 percent of controlling ownership, and any type of business can potentially qualify.

Immigration officials will want to confirm that you can generate sufficient income to provide yourself and your family with a comfortable living in the U.S. You also have to create jobs for U.S workers—usually hiring at least two employees, not including the owner. They do give you time. They give new businesses a reasonable amount of time to reach profitability and create jobs. It must be an actively operating for-profit business.

How do you apply for a visa? You can try to do it yourself, but it's probably easier to pay an attorney to get it done. We have people who'll take care of everything for you. Generally, it requires a visa interview. In the past, it took one to three months of processing time. It may take more than that now. With Norma, we've been working on it now for about four months. Plan on being involved in the process itself for a few months.

You can process your application within the U.S., without leaving the country if you're already here. I worked with another gentleman, Kareem. He and his family were coming over here from the Middle East. It actually took them about a year and a half. He wasn't quite ready, but he was getting there.

Fortunately, the franchise he was looking at held his territory for him. He got into a tutoring franchise to get the E-2 visa. There are many franchises that work with E-2 visa candidates and will hold territories for them while they're going through the process.

THE EB-5 INVESTMENT GREEN CARD

An alternative to the E-2 visa is the EB-5 investment green card. The requirements recently changed, but it used to take about $1 million to get into the U.S. Now it takes about $1.8 million. There are different requirements if you're looking to go into a high unemployment area. If it's a targeted area, then about $900,000 will do—about half of that is what you need to invest to get into the U.S. on an EB-5 green card. You also need to create at least ten new full-time direct employment jobs for U.S. workers within two years.

If you want to get into a franchise, but you do not want to come to the U.S. and instead want to get it going in your own country—yes, you can do that. You can do a single unit or multi-unit franchises. Generally speaking, if you have a product that you want to distribute to people using a franchise system, franchises prefer you to either be an area developer or engage in master-type franchising.

You're going to set up the supply chain and be the right-hand person of the franchise so you can grow their business. You'll be doing all the training and mentoring of new franchisees in your country. It's much easier that way than the franchise going to your country to do all the work itself.

If the franchise is going to open up in another country where it hasn't been before, then it needs somebody who is familiar with all the systems, the bureaucracy of government, and how to get things set up there. The franchise helps you with everything, such as getting the supply chain set up, but it needs a strong businessperson who knows the rules and regulations for that area.

In general, some of the product-type franchises are looking for somebody to pick up a large territory and help them develop. Some franchises are already overseas. In that case, we have quite a few franchises that you can do. For some of the more service-type industries, especially when you do consulting services on the side or market tech services, you may not need to get a larger territory and you can do single units.

INTERNATIONAL IS POSSIBLE!

So, if you're interested in opening up a franchise business and you're in another country and you want to stay there, you can. One of the benefits of what I do is that I get to work with all sorts of interesting people all over the world and help them realize their goals and their dreams and change their lives for the better forever.

Go to franchisemaven.com and look under the visas. That will give you information on treaty countries and visa requirements. If you're franchising around the world, give me a call or send me an email and let's connect to go over which franchises are available in the country you are in.

With Norma, we found her a nice visa attorney who does everything, got the business plan set up, and got the visa taken care of. It's been six months since we started working together, and within the next couple of months she will be in sunny San Diego.

CHAPTER 10

PROVIDING FREEDOM

(ARE YOU LOOKING TO FRANCHISE YOUR BUSINESS?)

Jerod and Dustin started their senior-care business, called A Place at Home, back in 2012. They were originally motivated to take care of their grandparents and great-grandparents. While they always thought they would eventually scale their business, when they first started, they weren't too sure what that would look like. They just knew they wanted to help others.

A Place at Home grew, and their clients kept asking for more services. So, they continued adding more services. Any thoughts of scaling continued, based on natural expansion. Eventually they needed to come up with a business plan and pro forma statements covering their earnings, without certain nonrecurring expenses. It was time to be a little more deliberate about the company, rather than constantly adjusting to everyone's needs as they emerged.

Jerod had gone to business college, starting in 2003. His first impressions of franchising were formed therein. Unfortunately, his impression of the idea was that he would lose control of locations run by franchisees—as opposed to opening more units personally. Nevertheless, he wasn't receiving a great deal of positive information about franchising or franchises. Later, he received no information to counter that at the university where he completed his MBA program. But he found himself thinking about the validity of franchising and the benefits it might have after growing A Place at Home with Dustin.

Jerod saw other business owners franchising their businesses. I can tell you, throughout the U.S. that remains the case. Jerod and Dustin figured they could too! Jerod just needed to make certain that they were doing it differently than everybody else in the senior-care industry—which had a lot of players in it already. So, he got to work researching about franchising and solidifying their core differentiators.

JEROD'S OWN WORDS:

"We weighed the pros and cons of growing our business internally by adding locations and creating a management hierarchy to scale the business. This is the traditional way of growth and the way I was taught in college to grow a business. Ultimately, if we were to provide the best possible service and the best possible chance for that location to succeed, we needed to franchise. We needed business owners who have a face to the business and stake in the game. They would do what it takes to be successful and provide the best possible care."

As I recommend throughout this book, it's always good to get professional help from people who know more about any particular subject. Jerod and Dustin had joined the International Franchise Association (IFA). They then got started learning as much as they could about becoming successful franchisees. When Jerod finally did get a model for it, he saw how he could become a franchisor.

Before finding any franchisees and opening new units, Jerod and Dustin would need to sort out the details, including getting advice on legal considerations (ultimately, a franchise-specific attorney group was retained). These were the key factors they needed to address:

- Current role and needs
- Ability to remove themselves from day-to-day tasks
- Policies and procedures
- Market analysis
- Money
- Their ideal franchisee

CURRENT ROLES AND NEEDS

A Place at Home had a couple of locations open and had managers in place. Of course, getting those in place came with some concern. For instance, if you receive a call about a new client on a Friday evening when everyone is ready to go home for the day, a manager who's paid hourly isn't likely to want to stay any longer or work through the weekend, signing up and assigning staff for the new client. However, an owner (or franchisee) would have much more stake in the game. When that's the case, staying longer for a new client is all about securing a new income stream. In Jerod and Dustin's case, it is about making sure a senior receives care when needed. Ideally, this means people in such a role would not be turning down business on a Friday night.

Jerod was able to see that additional units or locations would be in better hands if they had franchisees who had stake in the game who cared about the quality of service provided and the satisfaction of their staff. Now that they had a better idea of how franchisees would be involved, they would need to solidify their policies and procedures. This required them to take a step back so they could have more time to prepare everything.

DISTANCE FROM DAY-TO-DAY TASKS

A Place at Home was already profitable. It was already growing, but they needed to find out how they would remain profitable without having to directly run the business. They had to remove themselves from day-to-day operations and work toward releasing some control over their additional units.

This required some help, and good systems were essential. Senior care is super-competitive, and having ideal systems in place could help them push the envelope. To accomplish this, they researched many different operational systems to see what best fit their style of management and leadership. This allowed them to narrow in on key performance indicators (KPIs), key roles, tasks, and specific numbers for all of their franchisees to follow. They also had to come up with a solid vision on growth, which they did.

"You need to change your mindset when franchising. You need to shift your focus from selling the goods or services that your business offers to awarding franchises." —Jerod

POLICIES AND PROCEDURES

The language in Jerod and Dustin's current policies and procedures had to change a bit. The new language had to encompass franchisees taking over, rather than what had been required just for hiring a manager. They needed some help to do that, so they went to the IFA to find people who could help them create the right language and documents. Please note, there are many franchise-development teams out there. You can contact me at any time for more information on the various teams that will turn your business into a franchise.

Nevertheless, Jerod and Dustin needed to transform their manager's office manual into a franchisee manual. They needed to make a road map to launch units and map out everything that would be provided to or done for franchisees by A Place at Home.

MARKET ANALYSIS

Now that they were looking into growing their business, they required a market analysis. They needed to look at which markets their business would do well in and in which ones it wouldn't. They needed to figure out how well their services would perform in the various markets where they could start offering franchise units.

They also had to factor in the senior-care franchising market. As mentioned before, this industry is competitive. They needed to see what they were going up against. Also, they needed to make sure they were remaining competitive in terms of royalties, fees, territory sizes, education, and other factors that their competitors were offering.

Again, discussing topics like this with multiple experts is essential. Beyond discussion, there are plenty of folks who can do market analysis for you. You don't need to do this alone. Jerod and Dustin had the right people involved, and this helped them secure the future they wanted.

MONEY

And, of course, to realize their vision, they needed money. Creating a franchise already costs money, obviously; turning it into a growing franchise does too. Expanding the total number of units for management already requires investment. Eventually, the advantage with franchisees is that those new players enter the game with funding. If you can set this up well, your franchise will be ready to receive the right people.

This is my next point: they had to start thinking about who their ideal franchisee would be. What kinds of people would share their values? After doing some work on their values and mission statement, they needed a marketing budget to reach the right people for the job.

Before Jerod and Dustin could bring on franchisees, they needed to solidify everything, which would require money—be it for experts involved, software, resources, marketing to potential franchisees, and so on. They put their handbooks and policies together and created a business plan for the franchise system. They approached investors, friends, and family. They already had a profitable location and good bank relationships. They pitched it to private equity investors as well. In the end, they got the funding they needed.

IDEAL FRANCHISEE

When everything was under way, Jerod and Dustin interviewed many different people who had been directed their way via marketing. Eventually, they found ones they liked. There are many different ways to market your franchise to potential franchisees—which needs to be done in order to grow your franchises. Of course, you can do it personally, which involves organic traffic—which can be slower than you might like.

There are many different companies that will help you advertise your franchise on various portals. People can then search on the internet, find it, click on it, and ask for more information. Brokered groups, as well as franchise development groups, can also do this for you.

There are a few variables to measure when it comes to this aspect of turning your business into a franchise. One of them is whether you want to have inside sales—as in, will you employ a salesperson? Costs will definitely start adding up, and at some point you might find that it's worth going with the cost of having a development team or broker group to do this for you. For more on the various costs, don't hesitate to reach out. You can also visit my website: franchisemaven.com.

"You might be dissuaded from franchising because you think that your business isn't perfect, and you don't have all the answers. The truth is, no business is ever perfect, nor do they ever have all the answers. You will learn along the way, and we continue to grow and learn from every franchisee and location we develop." —Jerod

Jerod and Dustin found a few different companies with services they thought would be better than others. And, in fact, those companies managed to find hundreds of leads, but they narrowed them down to a smaller group. After some initial interviews, Jerod and Dustin started finding people who could be a great fit for their franchise.

Narrowing down the ideal franchisee is essential. As you might recall from the movie *The Founder* (starring Michael Keaton), when Ray Kroc initially franchised McDonald's, he thought he knew who he was looking for—any given investor who would be interested. However, he then discovered that married couples were the ones who held his values and could hold to the way he wanted the franchise to run.

It's well worth the time to find the right fit. And Jerod and Dustin did just that, interviewing quite a few people. They soon found that they liked healthcare, service, military, and hospitality people, and focused on the ones who shared their values. Jerod and Dustin also looked for track records of success in the careers of their potential franchisees in the areas of management, sales, and operations.

Beyond getting leads, they wanted to personally take potential franchisees through the process themselves. They did that without hiring anybody else at that point in time. They still ran their A Place at Home, too, which obviously kept them very busy. Once the franchisees came on board, both of them helped each one launch their new business.

But let's take a break! I'll share more about their journey at the end of the chapter. For now …

IS YOUR BUSINESS READY? (ASSESSING WHETHER YOU CAN FRANCHISE YOUR BUSINESS)

Let's talk about you! Maybe you have a business you want to grow. You've worked hard to build your business. It is your baby. And maybe you've already expanded from one unit. But where do you go from here?

Well, putting up new units yourself is doable; however, you're using your own money and time. Of course, you get to keep all the profit for yourself—which we can consider linear growth. But perhaps you want to move faster or exponentially. We call this franchising.

Franchising means transitioning from servicing your customers as a business owner or chairperson to now servicing your franchisees. It's important that you have a plan, as we established with Jerod and Dustin. They had some plans, but many of their plans developed as they moved along. Let's take a little time to see what this might look like for you and your business. Is your business ready for franchising to markets?

First off, do you have one location—or have you tried opening up your business in other markets as well? If you haven't, this requires some analysis. Jerod and Dustin had other people assist them to gather data.

What data do you have that shows your business will work in other markets? Is the product or service universal? Will anybody, anywhere, need it or want it? Obviously, for A Place at Home, senior care works well just about anywhere. We regularly have people who are getting to that age when they need help around the house, and that service can be used anywhere. Areas with more seniors in the population would be the most profitable, of course.

Also, what's unique about your business? What sets you apart from your competition that will help you find more potential franchisees? One thing that Jerod and Dustin focused on was their differentiators, or what unique offerings they could provide that other senior-care franchises did not. So, think about why your clients are coming to you instead of another company—and capitalize on that! Beyond data, money will be needed to secure your transition. Generally speaking, just to get the franchise created, you're probably looking at around $100,000. It varies from business to business.

As always, I recommend joining the IFA so you can interview different companies to find out what they charge and what they'll do for you for that money. Then you can determine your best way forward. When someone is creating a franchise for you, you'll be looking at franchise disclosure documents, franchise agreements, policies and procedures, manuals, and registration in various states. In the end, this will allow you to offer franchises in the U.S.

Something you should definitely think about is your vision. Doing this enabled Jerod and Dustin to find people who could help them get where they wanted to go and find potential franchisees who matched their values. So, what's your vision? World domination is a good vision to have, of course. Are you looking at any particular cities or markets? As an example, perhaps you want to put a reading center in every city in the U.S.

I recommend writing your vision down as soon as it strikes you. And think about your core values. Sharing those with potential franchisees and having the buy-in from them will be essential down the line.

FUTURE CHECKLIST (FROM PRIVATELY OWNED BUSINESS TO FRANCHISE)

I want to take you through a short checklist to get you thinking about your plans for the future. Here we'll look at the following variables:

1. Territory size
2. Ideal franchisee
3. Target states
4. Support plans
5. Selling franchises
6. Your ultimate goal

TERRITORY SIZE

How many potential customers will your franchisees need in order to generate a certain amount of money?

For example, let's take another look at the senior-care business. Generally speaking, your senior-care franchise will give you around 30,000 seniors as a territory size—whatever that encompasses geographically. So as far as territory goes, this will determine how you can apply exclusive rights to a market and serve clients in given areas—meaning you can't sell units in that territory once a franchisee has become operational there.

For senior care, a territory can be determined by the total population of potential clients served as well as by income levels. If you're looking at a bricks-and-mortar franchise, for the most part they use a mile radius, since people probably look for the closest one that fits their needs—meaning they won't likely drive out of their way to find a location.

Have you determined which markets will work and which markets won't? And does every market need what you are selling? Or do you have to be specific to certain areas?

IDEAL FRANCHISEE

Who is your ideal franchisee? Jerod and Dustin thought they had a good idea of who it was at first. Then, once they started bringing in new potential franchisees, they refined their ideal a bit. Most likely, your ideal will probably go through some refining as well. Again, Ray Kroc eventually realized his ideal franchisee was actually a team of spouses—and really, owner-operators rather than just basic investors.

You're looking for people who will share your vision and core values. This is especially essential if you use outside consultants like me to help you grow your franchise. You tell us who you are looking for, and we go find those people for you.

Some of the franchises we work with are looking for people with good business backgrounds, who know how to grow a business, how to find managers, and how to develop teams. That's a central part of their business. But it always varies according to the franchise, and it will vary according to what you're looking for.

TARGET STATES

What states do you want to sell in? Not all states are created equal! Some require more paperwork and more fees than others. In terms of senior care, some states actually have moratoriums on the number of senior-care businesses that are allowed. In something like home improvement, general contractor work, you need to know which states require specific licenses.

Are you producing a product that you want to keep control over for quality reasons? If that's the case, if you need everything to be developed and come out of your central location, how is that going to work logistically? Well, when you start growing, perhaps you need to stay closer to home at first. Keep the shipping costs down until you can develop better ways around another place where you can develop your product.

We have franchisors using the above strategy. They want to expand in the north until they reach a certain level of franchisees. Otherwise, the shipping costs would cut far too deep into profits, and locations farther away would not be viable.

SUPPORT PLANS

What is your plan for supporting your franchisees? Again, as we all learn eventually, you can't do everything. You've got to have some people who are going to help you out. As you grow, you will need to create a development team.

So, how many people will you need in the home office to support these franchisees? Who will be in charge of what? Get a feeling for that. Know your numbers. Know the titles of the employees and how many you'll need. And this brings us to our next point …

SELLING FRANCHISES

How do you plan on selling your franchise? First off, we refer to this as "awarding the opportunity to invest" in your franchise. You are awarding people the opportunity; you are not "selling" a franchise to just anyone. For readers looking to find a franchise, and if you are a good fit for one, you will be awarding the franchise the opportunity to use your skill set—and the franchisees will benefit from this because their business will expand. For those of you looking to create a franchise of your own, you are awarding your ideal franchisee the opportunity to use your skill set to help them grow. It's a two-way street. Keep this "awarding" at the forefront of your brain.

OK, so this is a real big one: you need to determine if you will have an inside sales team or if you must outsource sales—or both. This is what you will be doing: taking potential franchisees through the process of investigating your franchise to determine if the arrangement is a good fit for both of you. You may do it yourself to begin with. However, if the investigation process takes six to eight weeks, and I start bringing you two or three people per week, you are going to be talking to a lot of people every day and will not have time for anything else.

With Jerod and Dustin, they worked with every new candidate at first. They started using different services and ways of bringing people in as they grew. And then as they grew more and more, that's when they hired their sales development person.

YOUR ULTIMATE GOAL

What is your ultimate goal? You have your vision for growing the franchise (world domination), but what is your ultimate goal? Are you hoping to keep it as long as you feel like running it and then turn it over to your kids? Will you sell it? Jerod and Dustin are looking to create a legacy business to turn over to their kids, assuming the kids want it!

In my experience, private equity firms start looking at purchasing franchises once they get up to fifty to one hundred units. This is the point when the royalties make a franchise self-sustaining and are a good investment for private equity. Overall, it's important to have a vision and an endgame in mind.

A PLACE AT HOME TRANSFORMATION

Jerod and Dustin put together their onboarding process for franchisees from scratch. Again, they handled onboarding themselves while they continued running A Place at Home. What I didn't mention is that they put their own process together without anyone teaching them how to do it.

> "We got the advice from a fellow in-home care franchisor that when you franchise you need to plan on 10% franchisee turnover. If you are less than this, you are too strict in who you bring on. If you are over this, you are too lenient." —Jerod

While they worked with different professionals, including people from the IFA, they were able to learn everything they needed. Even though there were people who could pull everything together for them, that's not how they wanted to do it. They basically started with an Excel sheet. They used this to walk everyone through their list of tasks and progression timeline.

Soon enough, they figured out that this is pretty tough to do in Excel. So, they found a great software platform to follow and built the process on it. They found this really easy to rebuild every time that they needed to get a new franchisee started. Then they could just transfer it over. There were a lot of tasks, details about what they're responsible for, and a timeline of everything that goes on.

Obviously, they didn't want to just give somebody a list and say, "Go get 'em, Tiger! There you go!" Through their hard work and working with the right people, they were able to come up with a road map to find various vendors who could help them through that. When they had a few units open, they started focusing on replicating profitable results, along with successful policies and systems. The more they did this, the more effective and easier it would become.

Doing everything yourself quickly leads to the realization that there are way more moving pieces than you may have expected. Jerod and Dustin quickly figured out that they would need to come up with digital marketing people, web design people, marketing supplies, and more. Not only that, but all of this also then needed to be supplied to their franchisees to continue the franchise's success. And "all this" included:

- A website
- Web designers
- Digital marketing
- Marketing supplies (pamphlets and flyers)
- Customer satisfaction surveys
- Books management
- Licensing
- Insurance

- Phone systems
- Email platform
- Document storage, management, and sharing
- Payment processing
- Continuing education

You either need to develop all of that yourself or you can find someone to do it for you. As established, Jerod and Dustin eventually learned the advantages of doing the latter. They used the IFA to find vendors. They also found some attorney consultants. After working on these details, this further helped them to establish expectations for franchisees—a marketing budget, a vendor database (for marketing, especially), and a standard guide.

Again, this all came together along the way as they learned from owners, professionals, and vendors alike. They continued learning as they got deeper into the process. They were discovering the license requirements in various states and what needed to be done.

"Knowing your strengths will help you to solidify your role in the franchise business. Hire, contract, or find vendors to fill the gaps. Trying to be everything to everyone and putting it all on your shoulders will constrain your growth." —Jerod

As Jerod and Dustin were able to successfully improve the process of replication and onboarding, they began working with their broker and consulting network relationships. They were planning future growth to be better, and to improve their process with technology differentiators. They brought people up from within their ranks as well.

As established, support for franchisees requires people, so they brought in the following team:

- Director of Marketing
- Director of Business Performance
- Operational and Financial Support Specialist
- A marketing brand engagement specialist who launched sales, video services, care, recruiting, specialty programs, fall prevention, and training for caregivers
- Franchise Development Coordinator

Also, Dustin z(CEO) and myself (President)—I oversee Development and Dustin oversees the Operations.

This team grew as they awarded more franchisees and, by the time they had fifteen franchisees, A Place at Home had the above team in place. This team should support their growth to over forty locations. Now they're focused on growing their business further, whether in better support or services. They're finding improvements and opportunities to make everything easier. Because the infrastructure is in place, that means they have more time and energy to develop new services for the people they serve.

When last we spoke, the opportunity that they're looking at growing is a residential group home for seniors. This helps fulfill their mission to provide places for seniors who can no longer live in their own homes, as well as to help their current franchise owners have growth plans that can be supported by the infrastructure created in their A Place at Home business. We have sold our corporate locations to franchisees. We are now in the process of signing our 28th location. This franchise opportunity definitely plays a part in their endgame. And what they really want is to leave a legacy. If their kids want to take the businesses over, Jerod and Dustin want that to be a realistic possibility.

"Franchising your business is a long play. It is not a get-rich-quick plan. You are in it for the royalties and not the franchise fees. Explosive growth without a strategic growth plan is a recipe for a lawsuit." —Jerod

DON'T SETTLE FOR STRUGGLE

While Jerod and Dustin's journey was a good learning process, they look back and wish they had raised more money for their transition into becoming a franchise. They found that marketing is key. They surely saw the importance of understanding their ideal franchisee and being able to project their vision to them.

This doesn't always need to be a learning experience or a struggle. Similar to what I said in Chapter 2, it is important to talk to the right professionals at the right time (and talk to enough of them). My team and I work every day to bring people into franchising—and we turn businesses into franchises as well. We are ready to serve.

Reach out to me anytime you have questions about becoming a franchise. I know what potential franchisees look for in a franchise. I'll have a good idea whether your concept is something that I would or could put in front of my candidates. Visit franchisemaven.com at any time for more information, or feel free to just give me a call.

CONCLUSION

Before losing my corporate job, I had already started reading Robert Kiyosaki's books, and I realized there was a better path somewhere out there. As I shared in Chapter 1, I was always looking for challenges, and my corporate experience made me hungrier than ever before. But I was stuck in the age-old trap.

I think there's one good benefit that everyone can agree on with traditional jobs and it keeps people in that system: getting paid every two weeks or so is pretty cool. You don't even need to think about it. The money just pops right into your bank account, and you are good to go as long as you can put up with the atmosphere. Getting paid wasn't too painful, as long as it remained steady. But it was all so boring to me.

Part of the boredom was being so *in* the business that I wasn't part of the big picture. By itself, the work of being an engineer and doing the data analysis was really enjoyable. That's why it lasted about fifteen years for me, but I never necessarily felt like I was part of the big picture. I like working *on* the business. And I like growing the business itself and watching what happens when my decisions lead to success.

I'm glad Kiyosaki inspired me to engage in a semi-absentee business on the side. It took me back to my high school days and gave me a taste of the great life to come. Not only that, it showed me there was still something challenging and better-fitting for me outside of my corporate job.

As I was processing all of that, I'm absolutely certain that was the time when one of the managers realized what I already knew: my heart just wasn't in the work or in the environment. We were already facing layoffs, and I kept seeing it as a blessing when I wasn't hit by one. But I was wrong. The best thing that ever happened to me was getting laid off. It was a hard step. I think many employees find themselves addicted to the biweekly paycheck, and I was determined to kick that addiction.

I took the hard step. And let me tell you, there's definitely a big change when you're working *on* the business out here, and you're no longer one of the people working *in* the business. Finding ways to help that business grow is a big change. *In* the business, you're like a cog in a wheel, and they don't always share the big picture because they need you to be a cog. *On* the business, you are the wheel itself. And I forgot how much I loved the freedom of wheels …

My earliest mode as an entrepreneur was handling a paper route as a young boy. A lot of young folks back in my day were able to do this. I think that was one of the greatest things around. Back then, you could have your own business as a child without the responsibilities of adulthood! You would collect money by going door to door at the end of each month, and whatever money was left over after paying the paper was yours for the taking. And then you would pick up the papers and deliver them on your own time—for me that was in the afternoon, after I was done with school.

I was collecting for the *Daily Democratic*. It was my very first job and the first time I had money of my own. Keeping that business going was the greatest feeling in the world. I was doing something on my own, making a profit, and I had money in my pockets. I didn't have a mortgage or a family to support. I was just a kid, and I would spend money on comic books and candy—as long as Mom and Dad were OK with those things, of course.

So, when I started getting my own businesses with the dry cleaners, then the storage units, and then the rental properties, it took me back even further than high school. I was thirteen or fourteen all over again. They were my businesses. I was riding the bike all over again, after school. And when it was time to see the ROI—*Right on!*—it was like being at the comic book shop again at the end of the month. Of course, now that I'm grown, my money goes to different things.

REAL FREEDOM

My wife and I have been married for about thirty years. We've always had gardens, chickens, and pheasants. And we always tried to grow as much as we could ourselves. We've always liked the mountains and the idea of being far enough away that we could be a little bit secluded while living off the land.

We wanted to be as self-sustaining as possible, but not for anything weird like the world coming to an end or a zombie apocalypse—we just liked the idea of being able to produce our own food. Well, that was until we actually lived that dream. When we went up into the mountains of New Mexico, we came to realize that living on a snow-covered hill meant being excluded and isolated. On top of that, it was really hard to grow stuff at 8,000 feet.

We did that for about a year. Then we went down a few thousand feet to get a longer growing season. It was the right adjustment. When I was working in Texas, in my old corporate life, we had about 10 acres. In New Mexico, we were able to expand to 65 acres. In our new life together, we were able to find another 160 acres in Missouri. Now we have plenty of room to do what we want and an environment to grow as much as we want.

As I found real freedom, I was able to pay cash to buy our land without a mortgage. I can't tell how great that feeling was. And it's an even better feeling to make our property self-sustaining—with fruit trees, a vegetable garden, and chickens. Out here, we're also able to attract wildlife to the area, which means we can harvest deer and turkey.

I may as well be a young boy on my bicycle again. My wife and I live our life on our terms. We have our "comic books and candy," and we only feel freer by the day. I can't wait to help more people accomplish this for themselves.

So, congratulations for getting this far and taking the next step toward your dream life. As we've gone through this book, I've shared stories of other people who have gone through the process with me, found franchises, and realized that their freedom is just one franchise away. Have you found that you related to any of the people in my stories? Do you have the same background as one or more of them?

Any good franchise consultant will help you realize your goals and expectations. I probably would have still been in that analysis paralysis—trying to go through all the different franchises I was looking at and attempting to figure out which should be the best. I talked to my franchise consultant to help me determine what to do.

If you feel we can work together toward your dream life, connect with me at franchisemaven.com. There's a link to my calendar to schedule a time to talk. You can ask me any question you want, and you can get to know me.

After that, if you are still interested, we'll have you fill out a questionnaire and I will send you background information on me and the team I work with so you can check us out as well. I'll make my franchise matches for you, and we'll work together so that you can make an informed decision on whether franchising is right for you—and, if it is, which one is the best fit.

Thank you very much for reading my book. I appreciate the time you've taken so far, and I wish you well as you dream of freedom. It's just one franchise away, and I am here to change your life for the better.

—Greg Mohr
franchisemaven.com

ABOUT THE AUTHOR

Greg Mohr started his work life in the restaurant industry. His first impression of franchising came straight out of high school, at a fast-food restaurant chain. He later managed a twenty-four-hour restaurant—another chain outlet but not a franchise. Seventeen years of restaurant management flew by before he earned degrees in electrical engineering and physics and became an engineer.

Greg climbed the corporate ladder, working in the semiconductor industry for about fifteen years. During this time, he earned an MBA specializing in management information systems. Doing so did not speed up his pace of climbing the ladder, as he had hoped. In the meantime, inspired by many business books, including Robert Kiyosaki's *Rich Dad, Poor Dad* series, Greg purchased rental properties and found that he could manage them on the side while keeping his day job.

As he loves to share, Greg eventually found himself laid off, and it was a blessing. He saw an opportunity and knew it was now or never. After working with a franchise consultant, he found a great fit after narrowing down his goals and criteria. He never looked back. Today, he helps others find their way on the same path at Franchise Maven (franchisemaven.com).

Made in USA - North Chelmsford, MA
68378_9781956649451
02.05.2024 2043